W9-BSA-700

CONUNDRUM

BY THE SAME AUTHOR

AS I SAW THE U.S.A.
SULTAN IN OMAN
SOUTH AFRICAN WINTER
THE HASHEMITE KINGS
THE WORLD OF VENICE
THE ROAD TO HUDDERSFIELD
THE PRESENCE OF SPAIN
(*with Evelyn Hofer*)
CITIES
OXFORD
PAX BRITANNICA
THE GREAT PORT
PLACES
HEAVEN'S COMMAND

JAN MORRIS

CONUNDRUM

A HELEN AND KURT WOLFF BOOK

HARCOURT BRACE JOVANOVICH, INC., NEW YORK

Printed in the United States of America

Library of Congress Cataloging in Publication Data
Morris, Jan, 1926-
Conundrum.
"A Helen and Kurt Wolff book."
Autobiographical.
1. Morris, Jan, 1926- 2. Change of sex—Personal narratives. I. Title.
CT788.M637A33 301.41'5 [B] 74-525
ISBN 0-15-122563-X

First edition
B C D E

ACKNOWLEDGMENTS

I owe my thanks to all those who, by reading my book in early drafts, acted as guides or bearers in this self-exploration —but especially, of course, Elizabeth and Mark, who knew the terrain as well as I did, and often spotted the route sooner.

The quotations from Dr. Robert Stoller come from his book *Sex and Gender*, Science House, New York, 1968. The C. S. Lewis passage is from *Perelandra*, Macmillan, New York, 1965. The verses by Cecil Day Lewis are from *Overtures to Death*, Jonathan Cape, London, 1938.

CONTENTS

This book describes a tangle in my life, and parts of it have been painful to write. Happy as I am by disposition, disinclined to self-analysis, and exceedingly lucky in all other respects, I have found it hard to rake over old torments and ambiguities. I have done my best, though, to make it an honest self-appraisal, and at least cheerfulness keeps breaking in. Where there are omissions, they are generally to spare other people distress, and only occasionally to save myself from chagrin. Where there are evasions, they are aesthetic rather than secretive. If the whole fable is blurred in a suggestion of arcanum, that it is because I see it so. I offer it diffidently, like a confidence: in love to my family, in explanation to my friends, and in sympathy to all my comrades, anywhere in the world, who are suffering still in the same solitary and unsought cause.

J. M., Bath, 1973

CONUNDRUM

ONE

UNDER THE PIANO · ABOVE THE SEA TRANSSEXUALITY · MY CONUNDRUM

I was three or perhaps four years old when I realized that I had been born into the wrong body, and should really be a girl. I remember the moment well, and it is the earliest memory of my life.

I was sitting beneath my mother's piano, and her music was falling around me like cataracts, enclosing me as in a cave. The round stumpy legs of the piano were like three black stalagmites, and the sound-box was a high dark vault above my head. My mother was probably playing Sibelius, for she was enjoying a Finnish period then, and Sibelius from *underneath* a piano can be a very noisy composer; but I always liked it down there, sometimes drawing pictures on the piles of music stacked around me, or clutching my unfortunate cat for company.

What triggered so bizarre a thought I have long forgotten, but the conviction was unfaltering from the start. On the face of things it was pure nonsense. I seemed to most people a very straightforward child, enjoying a happy childhood. I was loved and I was loving, brought up kindly and sensibly, spoiled to a comfortable degree, weaned at an early age on Huck Finn and *Alice in Wonderland*, taught to cherish my animals, say grace, think well of myself, and wash my hands before tea. I was always sure of an audience. My security was absolute. Looking back at my infancy, as one might look back through a windswept avenue of trees, I see there only a cheerful glimpse of sunshine—for of course the weather was much better in those days, summers were really summers, and I seldom seem to remember it actually raining at all.

More to my point, by every standard of logic I was patently a boy. I was James Humphry Morris, male child. I had a boy's body. I wore a boy's clothes. It is true that my mother had wished me to be a daughter, but I was never treated as one. It is true that gushing visitors sometimes assembled me into their fox furs and lavender sachets to murmur that, with curly hair like mine, I should have been born a girl. As the youngest of three brothers, in a family very soon to be fatherless, I was doubtless indulged. I was not, however, generally thought effeminate. At kindergarten I was not derided. In the street I was not stared at. If I had announced my self-discovery beneath the piano, my family might not have been shocked (Virginia Woolf's androgynous *Orlando* was already in the house) but would certainly have been astonished.

Not that I dreamed of revealing it. I cherished it as a secret, shared for twenty years with not a single soul. At first I did not regard it as an especially significant secret. I was as vague as the next child about the meaning of sex, and I assumed it to be simply another aspect of differentness. For different in some way I recognized myself to be. Nobody ever urged me to be like other children: conformity was not a quality coveted in our home. We sprang, we all knew, from a line of odd forebears and unusual unions, Welsh, Norman,

Quaker, and I never supposed myself to be much like anyone else.

I was a solitary child in consequence, and I realize now that inner conflicts, only half-formulated, made me more solitary still. When my brothers were away at school I wandered lonely as a cloud over the hills, among the rocks, sloshing through the mudbanks or prodding in the rockpools of the Bristol Channel, sometimes fishing for eels in the bleak dikes of the inland moors, or watching the ships sail up to Newport or Avonmouth through my telescope. If I looked to the east I could see the line of the Mendip Hills, in whose lee my mother's people, modest country squires, flourished in life and were brass-commemorated in death. If I looked to the west I could see the blue mass of the Welsh mountains, far more exciting to me, beneath whose flanks my father's people had always lived—"decent proud people," as a cousin once defined them for me, some of whom still spoke Welsh within living memory, and all of whom were bound together, generation after generation, by a common love of music.

Both prospects, I used to feel, were mine, and this double possession sometimes gave me a heady sense of universality, as though wherever I looked I could see some aspect of myself—an unhealthy delusion, I have since discovered, for it later made me feel that no country or city was worth visiting unless I either owned a house there, or wrote a book about it. Like all Napoleonic fantasies, it was a lonely sensation too. If it all belonged to me, then I belonged to no particular part of it. The people I could see from my hilltop, farming their farms, tending their shops, flirting their way through seaside holidays, inhabited a different world from mine.

They were all together, I was all alone. They were members, I was a stranger. They talked to each other in words they all understood about matters that interested them all. I spoke a tongue that was only mine, and thought things that would bore them. Sometimes they asked if they might look through my telescope, and this gave me great pleasure. The instrument played an important part in my fancies and conjectures, perhaps because it seemed to give me a private insight into distant worlds, and when at the age of eight or nine I wrote the first pages of a book, I called it *Travels With a Telescope*, not a bad title at that. So I was always gratified when after a few preliminary banterings—*"That's a big telescope for a little boy! Who are you looking for—Gandhi?"*—they wanted to try it for themselves. For one thing I was a terrible swank, and loved to focus my lens for them deftly upon the English and Welsh Grounds lightship. For another, the brief contact of the request made me feel more *ordinary*.

I was intensely self-conscious, and often stood back, so to speak, to watch my own figure stumbling over the hills, or sprawled on the springy turf in the sunshine. The background was, at least in my memory, brilliant and sharp-edged, like a Pre-Raphaelite painting. The sky may not always have been as blue as I recall it, but it was certainly clear as crystal, the only smoke the smudge from a collier laboring up-Channel, or the blurred miasma of grime that hung always over the Swansea valleys. Hawks and skylarks abounded, rabbits were everywhere, weasels haunted the bracken, and sometimes there came trundling over the hill, heavily buzzing, the daily de Havilland biplane on its way to Cardiff.

My emotions, though, were far less distinct or definable. My conviction of mistaken sex was still no more than a blur, tucked away at the back of my mind, but if I was not unhappy, I was habitually puzzled. Even then that silent fresh childhood above the sea seemed to me strangely incomplete. I felt a yearning for I knew not what, as though there were a piece missing from my pattern, or some element in me that should be hard and permanent, but was instead soluble and diffuse. Everything seemed more determinate for those people down the hill. *Their* lives looked preordained, as though like the old de Havilland they simply stuck dogged and content to their daily routes, comfortably throbbing. Mine was more like a glider's movements, airy and delightful perhaps, but lacking direction.

This was a bewilderment that would never leave me, and I see it now as the developing core of my life's dilemma. If my landscapes were Millais or Holman Hunt, my introspections were pure Turner, as though my inner uncertainty could be represented in swirls and clouds of color, a haze inside me. I did not know exactly where it was—in my head, in my heart, in my loins, in my dreams. Nor did I know whether to be ashamed of it, proud of it, grateful for it, resentful of it. Sometimes I thought I would be happier without it, sometimes I felt it must be essential to my being. Perhaps one day, when I grew up, I would be as solid as other people appeared to be; but perhaps I was meant always to be a creature of wisp or spindrift, loitering in this inconsequential way almost as though I were intangible.

I present my uncertainty in cryptic terms, and I see it still as a mystery. Nobody really knows why some children, boys and girls, discover in themselves the inexpungeable belief that, despite all the physical evidence, they are really of the opposite sex. It happens at a very early age. Often there are signs of it when the child is still a baby, and it is generally profoundly ingrained, as it was with me, by the fourth or fifth year. Some theorists suppose the child to be born with it: perhaps there are undiscovered constitutional or genetic factors, or perhaps, as American scientists have lately suggested, the fetus has been affected by misdirected hormones during pregnancy. Many more believe it to be solely the result of early environment: too close an identification with one or the other parent, a dominant mother or father, an infancy too effeminate or too tomboyish. Others again think the cause to be partly constitutional, partly environmental—nobody is born entirely male or entirely female, and some children may be more susceptible than others to what the psychologists call the "imprint" of circumstance.

Whatever the cause, there are thousands of people, perhaps hundreds of thousands, suffering from the condition today. It has recently been given the name "transsexualism," and in its classic form is as distinct from transvestism as it is from homosexuality. Both transvestites and homosexuals sometimes suppose they would be happier if they could change their sex, but they are generally mistaken. The transvestite gains his gratification specifically from wearing the clothes of the opposite sex, and would sacrifice his pleasures by *joining* that sex; the homosexual, by definition, prefers to make love with others of his own sort, and would only alienate himself and them by changing. Transsexualism is something different in kind. It is not a sexual mode or preference. It is not an act of sex at all. It is a passionate, lifelong, ineradicable conviction, and no true transsexual has ever been disabused of it.

I have tried to analyze my own childish emotions, and to discover what I meant, when I declared myself to be a girl in a boy's body. What was my reasoning? Where was my evidence? Did I simply think that I should behave like a girl? Did I think people should treat me as one? Had I decided that I would rather grow up to be a woman than a man? Did some fearful legacy of the Great War, which ravaged and eventually killed my father, make the passions and instincts of men repugnant to me? Or was it just that something had gone wrong during my months in the womb, so that the hormones were wrongly shuffled, and my conviction was based upon no reasoning at all?

Freudians and anti-Freudians, sociologists and environmentalists, family and friends, intimates and acquaintances, publishers and agents, men of God and men of science, cynics and compassionates, lewds and prudes—all have asked me these questions since then, and very often provided answers too, but for me it remains a riddle. So be it. If I have evoked my childhood impressionistically, like a ballet seen through a gauze curtain, it is partly because I remember it only as in a dream, but partly because I do not want to blame it for my dilemma. It was in all other ways a lovely childhood, and I am grateful for it still.

In any case, I myself see the conundrum in another perspective, for I believe it to have some higher origin or meaning. I equate it with the idea of soul, or self, and I think of it not just as a sexual enigma, but as a quest for unity. For me every aspect of my life is relevant to that quest—not only the sexual impulses, but all the sights, sounds, and smells of memory, the influences of buildings, landscapes, comradeships, the power of love and of sorrow, the satisfactions of the senses as of the body. In my mind it is a subject far wider

TWO

LIVING A FALSEHOOD · THE NEST OF SINGING BIRDS · ON OXFORD · A SMALL LUMP · IN THE CATHEDRAL · LAUGHING

As I grew older my conflict became more explicit to me, and I began to feel that I was living a falsehood. I was in masquerade, my female reality, which I had no words to define, clothed in a male pretense. Psychiatrists have often asked me if this gave me a sense of guilt, but the opposite was true. I felt that in wishing so fervently, and so ceaselessly, to be translated into a girl's body, I was aiming only at a more divine condition, an inner reconciliation; and I attribute this impression not to the influences of home or family, but to an early experience of Oxford.

Oxford made me. I was an undergraduate there, and for much of my life I have owned a house there—doubly fulfilling my own criteria of possession by writing a book about the city too. But far more important, my first boarding school was there: the signs, values, and traditions of Oxford dominated my early boyhood, and were my first intimations of a world away from home, beyond my telescope's range. I have, I hope, no sentimental view of the place—I know its faults too well. It remains for me nevertheless, in its frayed and battered integrity, an image of what I admire most in the world: a presence so old and true that it absorbs time and change like light into a prism, only enriching itself by the process, and finding nothing alien except intolerance.

Of course when I speak of Oxford, I do not mean simply the city, or the university, or even the atmosphere of the place, but a whole manner of thought, an outlook, almost a civilization. I came to it an anomaly, a contradiction in myself, and were it not for the flexibility and self-amusement I absorbed from the Oxford culture—which is to say, the culture of traditional England—I think I would long ago have ended in that last haven of anomaly, the madhouse. For near the heart of the Oxford ethos lies the grand and comforting truth that there is no norm. We are all different; none of us is *entirely* wrong; to understand is to forgive.

I became a member of the University of Oxford in 1936, when I was nine years old, and my name will be found in the university calendars for that year. This is not because I was any kind of prodigy, but because I was first educated there at the choir school of Christ Church, a college so grand that its chapel is actually the cathedral of the Oxford diocese, and maintains its own professional choir. No education could leave a more lasting effect than this experience did on me, and I doubt if any other kind of school could have satisfied so curiously my inner cravings. A virginal ideal was fostered in me by my years at Christ Church, a sense of sacrament and fragility, and this I came slowly to identify as femaleness—"eternal womanhood," which, as Goethe says in the last lines of *Faust*, "leads us above."

In those days the Cathedral Choir School, housed in unlovely obscurity in a high-walled narrow lane in the heart of the city, was virtually limited to the choristers themselves—sixteen boys in all. We were a medieval establishment, and we lived medievally—a nest of singing birds in an Oxford attic. We could produce a cricket team, but were too few to play each other. We acted in plays, but small ones. Our school concerts were mercifully short. We were, so to speak, custom-built: we were there to sing sacred music in the cathedral of St. Frideswide (an Oxford saint elsewhere considered unreliable, I have since sadly discovered, if not actually fictional), and everything else was sacrificed to that end. Our education was adequate, but was necessarily spasmodic: for twice a day we must put on our mortar-boards, Eton collars, and fluttering gowns and walk in file across St. Aldate's to the cathedral—gratifyingly stared at by tourists, and sometimes passed rather comically in the opposite direction by a parallel line of policemen, clumping in single file, helmeted and heavy-booted, toward their headquarters down the road.

Educationalists now would probably be horrified, if they inspected the conditions of our schooling: we must have been among the smallest boarding schools in England, and obviously this cramped our intellectual style. I see my time there, though, as one of benign beauty. It has often been suggested to me that, in those post-Victorian years of the 1930s, conventions of the day might have distorted my sexual notions. Man was for hard things, making money, fighting wars, keeping stiff upper lips, beating errant schoolboys, wearing boots and helmets, drinking beer; woman was for gentler, softer purposes, healing, soothing, painting pictures, wearing silks, singing, looking at colors, giving presents, accepting admiration. In our family, as it happened, such distinctions were not recognized, and nobody would have dreamt of supposing that a taste for music, colors, or textiles was effeminate; but it is true that my own notion of the female principle was one of gentleness as against force, forgiveness rather than punishment, give more than take, helping more than leading. Oxford seemed to express the distinction in a way that Cardiff, say, or even London never could, and in responding so eagerly to her beauties I did feel myself succumbing to a specifically feminine influence. I still do, and from that day to this have habitually thought of Oxford as "she"—unctuously following the example, as a critic once sniffed, of the worst Victorian *belles-lettres*.

Much of the beauty was purely physical, and my pleasure in it was physical too. Every afternoon we would cross to our playing-fields in Christ Church Meadow, an oblong of meadow-land beneath the walls of Merton. I loved this place with rather the same vibrant surrender, I see in retrospect, with which the poet Marvell loved his garden:

Stumbling on melons, as I pass,
Ensnared with flowers, I fall on grass.

Three big chestnuts grew in the corner, and in the long damp grass beneath them I used to lie unobserved and ecstatic, in the heavy sweet-smelling hush of an Oxford summer afternoon. Frogs leapt about up there, and kept me amused; grasshoppers quivered on grasses beside my eye; the bells of Oxford languidly chimed the hours; if I heard somebody looking for me—*"Morris! Morris! You're in!"*—I knew they would not bother to look for long. Marvell thought the Garden of Eden must have been best when Adam walked alone there, and all my life I have felt in places, in landscapes as in cities, an allure that seems to me actually sexual, purer but no less exciting than the sexuality of the body. I trace this perverse but convenient emotion to those scented afternoons of cricket long ago:

> *The gods, that mortal beauty chase,*
> *Still in a tree did end their race . . .*
> *And Pan did after Syrinx speed,*
> *Not as a nymph, but for a reed.*

But other Oxford seductions were less obvious. I loved the *idea* of the place hardly less than the look of it. I loved its age and oddity, its ceremonials, its quirks and antiquities. I loved the massed banks of books so often to be glimpsed through college windows, and the faces of the remarkable men we saw around us every day—statesmen and philosophers at the High Table in Christ Church Hall, theologians stately as knights in the pulpit, wild scholars talking to themselves in High Street. I loved the Christmas parties arranged for us by the Canons of Christ Church in their great canonical houses facing Tom Quad. How tall the candles were then! How rich but wholesome the cakes! How twinkling the Regius Professors turned out to be, stripped of their awful dignities! What thrilling presents we were given—envelopes with Penny Blacks upon them, magnificent wax seals of Bishops or Chancellors! How happy the old clergymen's faces looked as, breathlessly piping our gratitude—"Thank you very much *indeed*, sir!" "It was *jolly* nice of you, sir!"—we last saw them nodding their good-byes, a little exhausted around the eyes, through the narrowing gaps of their front doors!

I did not really know the purposes of Oxford, nor did I think it necessary to inquire. It was sufficient in its presence, not something that must be defined or explained, but simply part of life itself. It seemed to me a kind of country, where people were apparently encouraged to pursue their own interests and pleasures in their own time and in their own way; and this view of a university as an ideal landscape, through whose thickets, hills, and meadows the privileged may briefly wander, is one that I hold to this day.

All these were heady influences upon a child in my state of awareness. They encouraged me in my sense of difference, and of purity. The school itself was sensible and unhearty: nobody called me sissy for my poetic poses, or thought me silly when I blushed to expose my private parts. I detested sports, except cross-country running, but nobody held it against me, and the more sensitive of the staff, I think, recognized some ambiguity in me, and did their best to temper it. One moment of empathy I remember still with a pang. I was in the matron's room one day, reporting for a dose of Angier's Emulsion, perhaps, or collecting some darned socks, when she suddenly took me by both my hands and asked if she could show me something. She said it with a sweet but serious smile, and I expected to see a family trinket from a jewel-box, or the photograph of some beloved. Instead she walked to the window, drew the curtains, and took off her dress. I can see her rather scrawny figure now, in a pink satiny slip, and hear her voice with its trace of rustic Oxfordshire to it—"There's no need to be embarrassed, dear, you've often seen your mother undressed, haven't you?"

I did not know what to expect when, taking my hand in hers, she slid it round her slithery waist to the small of the back. "There," she said, "feel there." I felt, and there beneath the satin was a small hard lump. "Did you feel it?" she whispered, kneeling on the floor in front of me, and taking my face between her hands. "What can it be, Morris? What do you think it is?" I was touched, and frightened, and proud to have been asked, all at the same time, and did my small best to comfort her. It was nothing, I boldly said, nothing to worry about at all. Why, it was only a little lump. You could hardly feel it. My mother often had lumps like that.

The headiest influence of all, though, was the influence of life within the cathedral. I have never been a true Christian, and even now wish the great churches of Europe were devoted to some less preposterous exercise than worship. I except, though, from my iconoclasm your true-blue English cathedrals, if there are any left, where the Book of Common Prayer survives untampered, where the Bible is still King James's version, where fiery brides keep their fingers crossed as they promise to obey, where the smell is of must and candles, where the hassocks have been embroidered by the Diocesan Mothers' Guild, where the clergymen's vowels are as pure as their musical intonation is shaky, where gold plate gleams beneath rose windows, where organists lean genially from their organ-lofts during the sermon, where Stanford in C, *The Wilderness* or *Zadoc the Priest* thunder through the arches on feast days, and where at the end of evensong the words of the Benediction come frail, half inaudible but wonderfully moving from the distant coped figure raising his hand in blessing before the high altar. All these conditions were satisfied to perfection during my childhood attendance at the cathedral of Christ Church, Oxford, and beneath the orison of their mysteries I brooded and wondered, day after day, about the mystery of myself.

Investigators into transsexuality often comment upon the mystic trappings in which it is likely to be clothed. The ancients frequently saw something holy in a being that transcended the sexes, and sympathetic friends have detected, in the heart of my own quandary, some sort of inspiration. I first felt it myself, profane or ludicrous though it may appear to skeptics, during my years in that cathedral. Every day for five years, holidays apart, I went to service there, and its combination of architecture, music, pageantry, literature, suggestion, association, and sanctity powerfully affected my introspections. I knew that building almost as I knew my own home; or rather I knew *part* of it, for out of sight beyond the choir stalls were chantries and chancels we seldom had cause to penetrate, alcoves which sprang into life only on particular days of ceremony, and were usually obscured in shadow, dimly hung with the gossamer ensigns of disbanded regiments, and sometimes shuffled into, as into anonymity, by lonely bowed figures in search of solitude. But the bright-lit circle around the choir stalls became as it were my own, and it was there more than anywhere that I molded my conundrum into an intent.

An ancient holy building is conducive to secrets, and my secret became so intermingled with the shapes, sounds, and patterns of the cathedral that to this day, when I go back there to evensong, I feel an air of complicity. I found a passing fulfillment in the building, in a kind of dedication. Over at the choir school I increasingly felt myself an impostor among my friends, and winced, silently but in pain, when people in their ignorant kindness expected me to be as the others. Even the matron, if I had returned her confidence with one of my own, would doubtless have sent me to bed early or prescribed Syrup of Figs—more or less the reaction, I may say, which I would find in medical circles for another couple of decades. I wondered sometimes if it were all a punishment. Could I perhaps have done something fearful in a previous incarnation, to be condemned in this way? Or would I be compensated in an existence to come, by rebirth as Sonja Henie or Deanna Durbin? At other times I thought it might all be resolved by suffering, and when I sat in the dentist's chair, or lay miserable in the sickroom, or was being urged to be first off the diving-board into the cold pool, I called into play arcane formulae of my own: often I was told how brave I was, and this told me something about the meaning of courage, for I was really ticking off each moment of unhappiness as a contribution towards my release—truly storing up treasures in heaven.

But during our daily hours at the cathedral, I could be myself. There I achieved some childish nirvana. Pink, white, and scarlet in my vestments, genuinely inspired by the music, the words, and the setting, I was not exactly a boy anyway, but had undergone some apotheosis of innocence to which I aspire even now—an enchantment less direct than my abandonment beneath the chestnuts, but more complete in its liberation. Perhaps it is how nuns feel. Certainly I felt sure that the spirits of the place approved of it, and perfectly understood my desires. How could they do otherwise? The noblest aspects of the liturgy aspired to what I conceived as the female principle. Our very vestments seemed intended to deny our manhood, and the most beautiful of all the characters of the Christian story, I thought, far more perfect and mysterious than Christ himself, was the Virgin Mary, whose presence drifted so strangely and elegantly through the Gospels, an enigma herself.

Elevated in this guileless if soppy way, I began to dream of ways in which I might throw off the hide of my body and reveal myself pristine within—forever emancipated into that state of simplicity. I prayed for it every evening. A moment of silence followed each day the words of the Grace—"The grace of Our Lord Jesus Christ, and the love of God, and the fellowship of the Holy Ghost, be with us all evermore." Into that hiatus, while my betters I suppose were asking for forgiveness or enlightenment, I inserted silently every night, year after year throughout my boyhood, an appeal less graceful but no less heartfelt: *"And please, God, let me be a girl. Amen."*

How He could achieve it, I had no idea, and I was doubtless as vague as ever myself about the details of my desire. I still hardly knew the difference between the sexes anyway, having seldom if ever seen a female body in the nude, and I prayed without reason, purely out of instinct. But the compulsion was absolute, and irrepressible, and those cathedral days seemed to give it a sacred encouragement. I felt that there were Powers waiting to help me, someday. I did not despair, and being by temperament a cheerful child, and by circumstance a lucky one, I conditioned myself to cherish my secret more as a promise than a burden. "I make myself laugh at everything," as Beaumarchais's Barber has it, "for fear of having to cry." I do not wish to imply that I imagined some godly purpose working itself out in me: it is merely that those influences of my childhood, those English tolerances, those attitudes and sensations of Oxford, those consolations of Christian form, wove their own spell around my perplexities, softening them and giving them grace. I suppose there may seem to you something grotesque in the transsexual impulse, but it has never seemed ignoble or even unnatural to me. I agree with Goethe.

THREE

SEX AND MY CONUNDRUM · IN THE HAYLOFT · GENDER AND BOLSOVER MA

I wondered occasionally if others might be in the same predicament, and once, choosing a particular friend at school, I tentatively began to explore the subject. It had occurred to me that perhaps mine was a perfectly normal condition, and that *every* boy wished to become a girl. It seemed a logical enough aspiration, if Woman was so elevated and admirable a being as history, religion, and good manners combined to assure us. I was soon disillusioned, though, for my friend deftly diverted the conversation into a dirty joke, and I withdrew hastily, giggling and askew.

That my conundrum actually emanated from my sexual organs did not cross my mind then, and seems unlikely to me even now. Almost as soon as I reached my public school, Lancing, I learned very accurately the facts of human reproduction, and they seemed to me essentially prosaic. They still do. I was not in the least surprised that Mary had been invested with the beauty of virgin birth, for nothing could seem to me more matter-of-fact than the mechanics of copulation, which every living creature manages without difficulty, and which can easily be reproduced artificially too. That my inchoate yearnings, born from wind and sunshine, music and imagination—that my conundrum might simply be a matter of penis or vagina, testicle or womb, seems to me still a contradiction in terms, for it concerned not my apparatus, but my *self*.

If any institution could have persuaded me that maleness was preferable to femaleness, it was not Lancing College. The Second World War had begun now, and the school had been removed from its magnificent Sussex home to a congeries of country houses in Shropshire. I expect it had lost much of its confidence and cohesion in the process: certainly after the glories of Oxford and the volatile generosity of home it was disappointingly unstylish, and nothing about the school excited me, or ever renewed my sense of sacrament.

I was not really unhappy there, but I was habitually *frightened*. The masters were invariably kind, but the iniquitous prefectorial system could be very cruel. I was constantly in trouble, usually for squalid faults of my own, and was beaten more often than any other boy in my house. A silly and wicked ritual surrounded a beating by the house captain. The basement room was shrouded in blankets or curtains, giving it a true ambiance of torture chamber, and all the house prefects attended. I used to be sick with fear, and feel a little queasy even now, thinking about it Thirty Years On. Nor was any discipline I was later to experience in the British Army, no bawling of sergeants or sarcasms of adjutants, anything like as terrifying as the regimen of the Lancing College Officers Training Corps, whose compulsory parades were held every Thursday afternoon. We wore uniforms from the First World War, and drilled with nineteenth-century rifles lately captured from the Italians in North Africa, and the slightest tarnish of a button, or the crooked wrap of a puttee, could bring savagery upon us. For twenty years or more I dreamt about the horror of those parades, and of the burning pale blue eyes of the cadet sergeant, approaching me expectant and mocking down the ranks (for if I was actually present, having failed to convince the authorities that I had sprained my ankle or developed a feverish cold, I was exceedingly unlikely to be correct).

I wanted no share in this establishment. I left Lancing as soon as I could, volunteering for the Army when I was seventeen, and contemplating my years there I remember only two positive pleasures. One was the pleasure of roaming the Welsh border country on my bicycle; the other was the pleasure of sex. When I wandered off among the brackeny hills, or explored the castles that guarded that long-embattled frontier, I was retreating into a truer and more private role than anything Lancing permitted; and when I thrilled to the touch of a prefect's strong hand surreptitiously under the tea-shop table, I was able to forget that he had flogged me the week before, and could be my true self with him, not the poor hangdog boy crying over the packing-case, but somebody much more adult, confident, and self-controlled.

I hope I will not be thought narcissist if I claim that I was rather an attractive boy, not beautiful perhaps, but healthy and slim. Inevitably, the English school system being what it is, I was the object of advances, and thus my inner convictions were thrown into an altogether new relief. It seemed perfectly natural to me to play the girl's role in these transient and generally light-hearted romances, and in their platonic aspects I greatly enjoyed them. It was fun to be pursued, gratifying to be admired, and useful to have protectors in the sixth form. I enjoyed being kissed on the back stairs, and was distinctly flattered when the best-looking senior boy in the house made elaborate arrangements to meet me in the holidays.

When it came, nevertheless, to more elemental pursuits of pederasty, then I found myself not exactly repelled, but embarrassed. Aesthetically it seemed wrong to me. Nothing fitted. Our bodies did not cleave, and moreover I felt that, though promiscuity in flirtation was harmlessly entertaining, this intimacy of the body with mere acquaintances was inelegant. It was not what the fan vaulting expected of me. It was not what my girl friends had in mind, when they spoke in breathless undertones of their wedding night. It was a very far cry from Virgin Birth. It was also worrying for me, for though my body often yearned to give, to yield, to open itself, the machine was wrong. It was made for another function, and I felt myself to be wrongly equipped.

I fear my suitors thought me frigid, even the ones I liked best, but I did not mean to be ungrateful. I was not in the least shocked by their intentions, but I simply could not respond in kind. We indulged our illicit pleasures generally in the haylofts of farms, or the loose field-ricks they still built in those days, and I think it a telling fact that of those first sexual experiences I remember most vividly, and most voluptuously, not the clumsy embraces of Bolsover Major, not the heavy breathing of his passion or his sinuous techniques of trouser-removal, but the warm slightly rotted sensation of the hay beneath my body, and the smell of fermenting apples from the barns below.

So this was sex! I knew it at once to be a different thing from gender—or rather, a different thing from that inner factor which I identified in myself as femaleness. This seemed to me, while germane indeed to human relationships, almost incidental to Bolsover's cavortings in the hay-rick—I was right too, for if Bolsover could not at that moment have cavorted with some nubile junior, he would undoubtedly have gone up there to cavort with himself.

To me gender is not physical at all, but is altogether insubstantial. It is soul, perhaps, it is talent, it is taste, it is environment, it is how one feels, it is light and shade, it is inner music, it is a spring in one's step or an exchange of glances, it is more truly life and love than any combination of genitals, ovaries, and hormones. It is the essentialness of oneself, the psyche, the fragment of unity. Male and female are sex, masculine and feminine are gender, and though the conceptions obviously overlap, they are far from synonymous. As C. S. Lewis once wrote, gender is not a mere imaginative extension of sex. "Gender is a reality, and a more fundamental reality than sex. Sex is, in fact, merely the adaptation to organic life of a fundamental polarity which divides all created beings. Female sex is simply one of the things that have feminine gender; there are many others, and Masculine and Feminine meet us on planes of reality where male and female would be simply meaningless."

Lewis likened the difference between Masculine and Feminine to the difference between rhythm and melody, or between the clasped hand and the open palm. Certainly it was a melody that I heard within myself, not a drum-beat or a fanfare, and if my mind was sometimes clenched, my heart was all too open. It became fashionable later to talk of my condition as "gender confusion," but I think it a philistine misnomer: I have had no doubt about my gender since that moment of self-realization beneath the piano. Nothing in the world would make me abandon my gender, concealed from everyone though it remained; but my body, my organs, my paraphernalia, seemed to me much less sacrosanct, and far less interesting too.

Yet I was not indifferent to magnetisms of the body. Some of the nameless craving that haunted me still was a desire for an earthier involvement in life. I felt that the grand constants of the human cycle, birth to death, were somehow shut off from me, so that I had no part in them, and could look at them only from a distance, or through glass. The lives of other people seemed more real because they were closer to those great fundamentals, and formed a homely entity with them. In short, I see now, I wished very much that I could one day be a mother, and perhaps my preoccupation with virgin birth was only a recognition that I could never be one. I have loved babies always, with the sort of involuntary covetousness, I suppose, that drives unhappy spinsters of a certain age to kidnap; and when later in life I reached the putative age of maternity, finding myself still incapable of the role, I did the next best thing and became a father instead.

What would Bolsover have said if, extracting myself from his loins, I had excused myself with these sophistries? But it all seemed plain enough to me. I was born with the wrong body, being feminine by gender but male by sex, and I could achieve completeness only when the one was adjusted to the other. I have thought about it for four decades since then, and though I know that such an absolute fulfillment can never be achieved—for no man ever became a mother, even miraculously—still I have reached no other conclusion.

erly pleased with themselves after chasing the Germans from Alamein to the Po. I liked them from the start, and short though my stay was with their ornate and swanky organism, retained an affection for it to the end—in 1960, when it was amalgamated at last with the 12th. After Italy I sailed with the 9th to Egypt and then, becoming the regimental intelligence officer, went with them to Palestine in the last years of the British mandate. They never treated me as one of themselves, and for this I was grateful: I was welcomed as a transient visitor from across some unmarked frontier, and this seemed apposite to me.

Soldiering has always paradoxically attracted me. Later I was to know militarism in very different circumstances, as I followed the armies of the West through the long rearguard action of imperialism, but miserable though this experience was, it did not quench in me a perverse respect for the profession of arms. I have always admired the military virtues, courage, dash, loyalty, self-discipline, and I like the look of soldiering. I like the lean humped silhouettes of infantrymen, and the swagger of paratroops, and all the martial consequence of embarkation or parade. Tanks in particular, which I used to know too well, have always fascinated me. They are, so I was taught at Sandhurst, no more than mobile guns: all their elaborate mechanisms of propulsion and control, all their tubes, brackets, and hatches, fulfill one purpose only, to get the gun to the right place, and shoot it straight.

Perhaps it is this very singleness of purpose that appeals to me, and I respond to soldiering because, being thinly plated myself, and lightly armed, I relish its brutal thrust. But in any case life with the 9th Lancers, in the years immediately after the Second World War, was soldiering in a less barbarous kind, and the insight it afforded me of life in an entirely male adult world was curiously gentle and considerate. The retreat from empire was only beginning then, unconsciously at that, and though we were inevitably drawn into one or two of the petty conflicts that were the imperial métier, still we had plenty of time, in Italy, Egypt, or Palestine, for the domestic side of military life.

For thoroughly domestic it was, in many ways, and there was an intimate beguilement to the affairs of such a corps. It was small—30 officers, perhaps, and 700 men. It was young. It was catty. Its members knew each other very well, and did not invariably like each other. The gulf between officers and men was deep and well defined: when years later I went back to write about the disbandment of the 9th Lancers, a sergeant told me that he thought the English class system to have been one of the secrets of such a regiment's long success—"it meant there was no envy, you see, it was all in the nature of things." I felt myself, though, to stand apart from this little hierarchy, and bore towards my own particular soldiers a responsibility less official than neighborly, perhaps; in return they entrusted me with tasks and intimacies which, I flatter myself, they would not have confided to all my colleagues (most of whom, I need hardly say, would have suffered at least as much for their troopers as they would for themselves).

Among the officers there was a powerful sense of family. It was hardly like being in an army at all. Age was disregarded and rank was tacit. Nobody called anybody "Sir." The colonel was Colonel Jack, or Colonel Tony. Everybody else was known by his Christian name. Courtesy towards each other was not a deliberate form, it was merely a matter of habit, or convenience. This was a very professional regiment. Wartime soldiers like me were a small minority, and many of them, too, had family connections with the 9th. A sense of heritage accordingly bound the officers one to another, and made us all conscious of lance and plume, saddle-carbine and cuirasse. These were the Delhi Spearmen; and though the details of the regimental history were less than vivid to most of us, still there hung always around our mess a general suggestion of glory (not that anyone would have been so insensitive as to mention it, for if there was one attribute the 9th Lancers were not anxious to display, it was *keenness*).

Assumptions of taste and behavior, too, could still in those days sustain such a company of men. The English world had not yet come apart, and a modicum of conformity was taken for granted. "Who was Jorrocks?" asked some ingenuous newcomer one day, during a pause in the 9th Lancers' favorite literary conversation—in those days every riding man knew the novels of Robert Surtees. There was a short staggered pause. "Who was *Jorrocks*?" an answering voice echoed incredulously. *"Where were you brought up, boy?"* Nobody minded if you pursued interests altogether your own; but it was generally understood that if you did not read Surtees, did not care much for horses, had not been to an acceptable school and would really rather be in the Royal Tank Regiment anyway, then at least you would have the sense and taste to keep quiet about it. Physical exhibitionism was tolerated, mental display was unpopular; the regiment was full of highly intelligent men, but the casual visitor might not have guessed it, for their conversation was deliberately muffled, and it was only in the seclusion of private talk that one tasted its real quality. This had always been so: among 9th Lancers of the past had been one officer who took his cello with him in order to play string quartets during the invasion of China in 1840, and another, upon his death in the 1950s, was said by *The Times* to have taken part in a cavalry charge, discovered a new species of Himalayan poppy, and translated the odes of Horace into excellent idiomatic English.

I invite my women readers to imagine how they would themselves have felt if, successfully disguised as a young man, they had been admitted to this closed and idiosyncratic male society in their late teens. For this is how I conceived my condition. The army had confirmed my intuition that I was fundamentally different from my male contemporaries. Though I very much enjoyed the company of girls, I certainly had no desire to sleep with them, and the sexual ambitions which so preoccupied the minds of my colleagues simply did not enter my head at all. My own libidinous fancies were far vaguer, and were concerned more with caress than copulation. I suppose I was really pining for a man's love. If so I suppressed the instinct; but as to my sense of gender, I knew it to be as different from that of my friends as cheese from chalk, or thump from serenade. I could not share the urgency of the male impulse, or the unquestioning sense of manhood which bound those soldiers together, and had carried them so bravely through so many ordeals.

You would find first, I think, if placed in the situation yourself, that it was extraordinarily *interesting*. Like a spy in a courteous enemy camp, or perhaps a dinner guest at one of the more traditional London clubs, you would find yourself caught up in the fascination of observing how the other side worked. For myself, I think I learnt my trade largely in the 9th Lancers, for I developed in that regiment an almost anthropological interest in the forms and attitudes of its society; and sitting there undetected, so to speak, I evolved the techniques of analysis and observation that I would later adapt to the writer's craft. I felt myself to be, as you would, totally separate and distinct: for I realized by now how deeply a male sexuality lay beneath their conduct, and how profoundly I lacked it.

You would also feel a sense of privilege. It was like eavesdropping by license. I am beginning to forget now what it was like to be able to sit as a man among men, and I shall never be in that position again; but even then I felt that I was lucky to have the experience. I was surprised that they should share their attitudes with me. In a curious way I was flattered that they accepted me. Sometimes nowadays I hear a party of men sharing a joke or an experience which, though not necessarily prurient, they would not think of sharing with a woman; and I think to myself not without a wry nostalgia that once long ago, in the tented mess of the 9th Queen's Royal Lancers, they would have unhesitatingly shared it with me.

But most of all you would have felt plain pleasure, at having handsome and high-spirited young men all around you. I did not realize it very consciously at the time, but this is undeniably what I felt myself. Cherishing my secret still, nevertheless I was encouraged often with indulgences, for by now, I discovered, both men and women sometimes instinctively felt the femininity within me. With women this gave me a new sense of ease, for it was always hard work pretending to be gallant; with men it gave me unexpected advantages. In the Army as at Lancing, I was never short of protectors. If my books were stolen, somebody would get them back for me. If I was losing an argument, somebody would back me up. If, at the training camp of the Royal Armoured Corps, I could not start my blessed motor-bike, I never had to kick for long. At Sandhurst I shared a room with a fellow-cadet who was willing, it seems to me now in wistful retrospect, to do for me any chore I wished, the more tedious, the more eagerly. The worst would never quite happen, I came rather smugly to think: somebody would always intervene, take the brunt, or forgive me. You know the feeling, I'm sure.

Such kindnesses were seldom exactly homosexual. I still did not look effeminate, and certainly did not feel myself to be homosexual. But the whole of English upper-class life, as I was later to discover more explicitly, was shot through with bisexual instinct. The public school system, the inhibitions of English manners, the happy tolerance accorded to originals and mavericks of every kind—all these traits meant that male relationships were full of emotional nuance and undertone. The great cavalry regiments of the old Army were no exceptions, and on the whole they preferred their young officers fresh and good-looking. It was a harmless quixotry, part a game, part I suppose a compensation, and if it ever went beyond the platonic I never experienced it myself.

Still it was there, even in the 9th Queen's Royal Lancers, the Delhi Spearmen, and it added to the warmth and piquancy of regimental life. I remember one officer complaining to me about the thickness of a subordinate's neck, an unfair aestheticism I thought to level at a perfectly competent tank commander, and once some of the subalterns had a quiz among themselves to rate their own order of good looks. Sometimes of course they womanized. I once escorted a nervous brother-officer to the doorstep of a brothel in Trieste, on his first excursion into the demimonde—how pale he stood there in the street light, looking back at me almost desperately, waiting for the door to open, as I drove away into the night! Sometimes they obeyed convention, flirted with rich Greek wives in Alexandria or sat aghast through the *exhibitions* of Port Said. Generally, though, they took their pleasures together, lived with a surprising abstemiousness, and seem to me in hindsight to have been engagingly naïve young men.

It was fun for me, it really was, to enter the wider world in such company. Would you not agree? In Italy we first learnt the delights of wine, as of opera. In Egypt we sampled the society of cosmopolitans—that shifting, glittering companionship of the Levant which still set the tone of Alexandria, with its pashas and its Greek panderers, its cotton knights and its Maltese entrepreneurs. In Austria we first encountered the Central European culture of which my mother, who had been educated in Leipzig, was herself truly a product, and whose poems and music had filled our house at home. In Palestine we consorted with clever Arabs of Jerusalem, and were entertained to tea by embittered patriots. It was a far Grander Tour than ever the milords experienced, and we were still scarcely more than adolescents. I can remember when, first arriving at Port Said off our troopship from Italy, a friend and I went out to dine at a restaurant in the town. "Good Heavens!" he cried, inspecting the wine list, "Rhine wines! How lovely it will be to taste them again after all these years!" I accepted his enthusiasm with respect at the time, but considering it now I realize that he must have been about sixteen years old when he had tasted them last.

Some of those evenings I remember with just the happiness, I suppose, with which a woman remembers her first evenings out with men, in the delicious gaiety of her girlhood. I remember for example the moment when, sitting with a brother-officer beside the window of a restaurant in Trieste, we saw two little urchin boys addressing themselves to us through the plate glass with that mummery of self-pity and appeal that was common then all over Europe—rubbing their little bellies to express hunger, wiping their eyes to simulate tears, holding hands to illustrate orphanhood, lifting their feet to display their broken shoes. They cannot have expected much from the well-fed young officers within, accustomed as they were to tips of a lira or two from the back of the hand, but on a sudden compassionate whim, which endeared him to me ever after, my companion took from his wallet some really valuable note, ten or perhaps twenty thousand lira in the inflated currency of the day, and sent it out to them by the waiter. They received it dumbly. They could not believe their eyes. They stared at it. They turned it over. They gazed at each other and at us. Then, suddenly realizing the full splendor of their windfall, as one boy they turned and leapt hilariously away down the street, dancing, skipping, flying almost, two little untidy blobs of arms, legs, flapping clothes, and tangled hair, laughing away out of sight towards the harbor.

And I relish still, as you may relish some intimate retreat of Chelsea or Greenwich Village, the duck-hunter's house at Grado into which the officers of the 9th had gained some privilege of access. It was the warmest, snuggest place imaginable. We would sit by the fire in the kitchen while the lady of the house prepared our meal, drinking grappa or red wine and practicing our Italian upon the duck man, and all around us the game-birds hung upside-down from their hooks, giving the room a still-life look, and making one feel deliciously insulated against the dank marsh outside. There were only oil lamps in the house, and when our soup was ready we would take the light with us to the table in the sitting room, and squeeze ourselves in at the white-clothed table against the wall. Our host would sit backwards on a chair beside us, to see us properly settled, and later sometimes his wife came in too, wiping her hands on her apron, to wish us *buon appetito*; but presently they left us with our roast duck, our wine, and ourselves, so that we sat there drinking, talking, and eating until the night was half gone, the lamp began to gutter and smell, and we must reluctantly tumble out of that best of clubs, that Pratts of the Veneto, into our truck and back to camp.

Best of all I remember my journeys and evenings with Otto, for I loved him. Half the Army knew Otto. He was one of the grand originals. His origins were mysterious, for he was fluent in German, had been briefly at Potsdam Military Academy, and claimed a maternal uncle who had been a German Field Marshal on the Russian front. Certainly he had access to a flat in Vienna, which he freely lent to his friends, and through whose keyhole, he pretended, elderly Hapsburg princesses used to peer to see the slim young Englishmen in their baths. Otto stuttered slightly, and was very brave: he had won a Military Cross for early exploits in flail tanks, devices which, demonically advancing through minefields whirling chains of steel in front of them, cleared a path for the armor and infantry behind. He was a small, slight man who walked in a stooped lopsided way, as though there were some maladjustment of his locomotion, and his expression was above all quizzical. I have a picture of him before me now, in a photograph of 9th Lancers officers taken on May 6, 1945, the last day of their long war: among all those tanned and vigorous English faces, smiling in success, his is thrust out pugnaciously, characteristically half in shadow, and his shoulders are hunched as though part-way through a shrug.

Otto did not stay long in the 9th Lancers after the war, drifting off to extra-regimental soldiering more to his taste. I heard of him from time to time—commanding a force of muleteers somewhere, accepting an improbable wager in Malaya—and finally he turned up as an officer of the Trucial Oman Scouts in the Persian Gulf; where, untypically pushing a captured Arab dissident into the back of a truck, he was stabbed for his discourtesy, and died of the wound. He died as he had lived, distinctively, but though I often meet people who remember him, still nobody seems to know much about his private life, and he is spoken of still with a vague and half-cynical affection.

When I knew him he was young and full of a saturnine charm. I loved the hint of wickedness that lay hooded and probably specious behind his fun. I loved his flaunted taste for the dissolute and the disreputable, which led some of our more proper colleagues, confronted by some appalling revelation over the dinner table, to respond with a stifled "Otto —*really*!" Otto was like an emissary from other existences outside, a foretaste of life as it might be when, freed from the military restraints, I could evolve styles and manners of my own. As regimental intelligence officer I had a jeep, and license to wander far and wide through the countries of the Fertile Crescent: on many of these long journeys Otto came with me, bringing his whisky and his repertoire of quotations from Omar Khayyam, and teaching me, from his long fighting experience in Africa, tricks of the desert trade.

At the same time he exemplified for me, more than anyone else in the regiment, the clublike brotherhood of men, which tantalized me, repelled me, and attracted me, all at once; for though his prejudices were brazen and his manners altogether his own, yet whether he was talking to general or corporal, Jewish scholar or Arab serf, a patrician in the Palazzo Grimani or a duck-hunter in the Grado marshes, he spoke to them in a vocabulary they instantly understood and accepted. He knew they would be on his wavelength, the cycle of maleness. I used to watch him with a sad admiration, and sometimes I caught from his eyes, as he exchanged badinage with the waiter or insults with the Cairo policemen, a flicker of understanding. Once late at night in the Suez Canal Zone, then a British military enclave, we were being driven cross-country back to camp at Qassassin. It was one of those stunning star-lit nights of an Egyptian winter, when the air smells only of sand and dryness, the sky looks so crisp you could cut it, and a brilliant chill makes your body shiver and your spirits soar. Otto and I stood in the back of the open truck, for the pleasure of the ride, leaning on the roof of the cab, and as we bumped across the open desert we stood closer together for warmth, and he threw a greatcoat over both our shoulders. We traveled for a time in silence, as the truck shuddered and jolted on, and then Otto spoke. "G-G-God," he said, "I w-wish you were a woman."

Reply came there none, as the night swept by; but dear God, I would answer him now.

Such was my substitute for girlhood, inadequate but rich in compensations, and this was the clash of sensibilities, inside and outside myself, which was to govern my emotions ever after. I loved the Army, but I could never be truly of it. I enjoyed my excursions into that male society, but I knew I could not stay. And while, as I say, in some ways I liked this observer's role, and came indeed to make a profession of it, still I pined sometimes to be a member *somewhere*. Just as, in possessing these two landscapes of my childhood, I had felt myself to belong to neither, so I felt now that I belonged to no segment of humanity. It is a fine thing to be independent in life, and a proud sensation to know yourself unique; but a person who stands all on his own, utterly detached from his fellows, may come to feel that reality itself is an illusion—just as the poor convicts of the nineteenth-century silence system, so isolated from their comrades that they were never allowed to see or hear another soul for years at a time, sometimes lost all grasp of their own existences, and became nonpersons even to themselves.

FIVE

IDENTITY · PRECEDENTS OF SORTS DR. BENJAMIN · "TO ALTER THE BODY!"

It is only in hindsight that I compare myself with those numbed and alienated prisoners. I was so blithe in many ways in my youth, and enjoyed so many advantages, that the conflict within me did not rage, but rather festered. I was subject to periods of melancholic depression, which grew fiercer as I grew older, but I looked on the bright side generally, and adhered to the belief, which I hold to this day, that self-analysis is often a mistake, and leads one only down endless and unprofitable paths of speculation. I did not query my condition, or seek reasons for it. I knew very well that it was an irrational conviction—I was in no way psychotic, and perhaps not much more neurotic than most of us; but there it was, I knew it to be true, and if it was impossible then the definition of possibility was inadequate.

I see now that, like the silent prisoners, I was really deprived of an identity. This is a trendy word I have long distrusted, masking as it often does befuddled ideas and lazy thinking. It is a nebulous word—even the Oxford Dictionary is uncertain of its derivation, and pragmatic about its meaning. I was reconciled to it, however, not long ago by a passage in *Eothen*, by my literary master Alexander Kinglake, in which he discusses the effect upon the traveler of a journey in the East. When Kinglake thought of identity, I would guess, he thought of the whole corpus of personality, how others saw him, what he considered himself to be, his status in the world, his background, his taste, his profession, his purposes. He thought of it, I am sure, as an entity—the fact of what one is. The dictionary collates it also with oneness, and with "the condition or fact that a person or thing is itself and is not something else."

Many people, when I have told them I am writing this book, have expressed the hope that it will throw light on "the mystery of identity," or "the search for identity," envisioning the human condition as a microcosm of universal truths. I do not think, though, in such cosmic terms. I conceive identity as Kinglake would have conceived it, and I realize now that the chief cause of my disquiet was the fact that I had none. I was not to others what I was to myself. I did not conform to the dictionary's definition—"itself and not something else."

The certainty of my conviction only raised more questions. How *could* I be so sure of my predicament? If I thought I felt like a woman, how could I know what a woman felt? What did I mean, when I said I was feminine? Was it really a personal matter at all, or were there confusions of identity that lay far outside the Freudian or the pathological, and had their roots in the state of the world? We were living in a twilight time. Old forces were dying and new energies emerging. Patterns that had seemed permanent were falling into chaos. Strange ideas sprouted everywhere. Could it be that I was merely a symptom of the times, a forerunner perhaps of a race in which the sexes would be blended amoebalike into one? The world was contracting fast, and its political and social divisions would inevitably fade. Confronted at last with its insignificance in the universal scale, might not mankind discard its sexual divisions too? Was this what I was all about? Or was there some chemic nostrum which, dispensed at the corner chemist under the National Health, and taken if possible with a glass of water, would in no time make me like everyone else?

When I left the Army I resolved to explore myself more deeply. Myth and history alike, I discovered, were full, if not of precedents, at least of parallels—men who lived as women, women who lived as men, hermaphrodites, transvestites, narcissists, not to speak of homosexuals or bisexuals. There is no norm of sexual constitution, and almost nobody has ever conformed absolutely to the conventional criteria of male and female. Through all the ages the idea of sexual overlap has fascinated poets and myth-makers, and it has also played its part in the great religions. God, said the Jewish chronicler, created man in his own androgynous image—"male and female created he them," for in him both were united. Mohammed on his second coming, says the Islamic legend, will be born of a male. Among Christians, Paul assured the erring Galatians, there was no such thing as male or female—"all one person in Christ Jesus." The Hindu pantheon is frequented by male-female divinities, and Greek mythology too is full of sexual equivocations, expressed in those divine figures who, embracing in themselves strength and tenderness, pride and softness, violence and grace, magnificently combine all that we think of as masculine or feminine.

It was, I think, the eighteenth century which first imposed

upon Western civilization rigid conceptions of maleness and femaleness, and made the idea of sexual fluidity in some way horrific. Perhaps it developed out of Protestantism, whose devotion to the patriarchal principle even forbade the cult of the Virgin Mary. Certainly earlier centuries did not require the male to be unyieldingly virile, or the female unremittingly demure, as Shakespeare's comedies happily demonstrate. There was more give and take in those days, it seems, the sexes mingled freely and easily, and the word "manly" had not acquired that intolerant connotation, that hint of cold bath and smoking-room caucus, which the Victorians were to give it (in older forms they made obsolete, it meant simply "human," or even "humane").

Other cultures too, ancient and contemporary, have freely recognized a no man's land between male and female, and have allowed people to inhabit it without ignominy. The Phrygians of Anatolia, for example, castrated men who felt themselves to be female, allowing them henceforth to live in the female role, and Juvenal, surveying some of his own fellow-citizens, thought the same plan might be adopted in Rome—*Why are they waiting? Isn't it time for them to try the Phrygian fashion, and make the job complete—take a knife and lop off that superfluous piece of meat?* Hippocrates reported the existence of "unmen" among the Scythians: they bore themselves as women, did women's work, and were generally believed to have been feminized by divine intervention. In ancient Alexandria we read of men "not ashamed to employ every device to change artificially their male nature into female"—even to amputation of their male parts.

Among more primitive peoples, so Sir James Frazer recorded in *The Golden Bough*, "there is a custom widely spread . . . in accordance with which some men dress as women and act as women throughout their lives. Often they are dedicated and trained to their vocation from childhood." The Sarombavy of Madagascar, for example, altogether forgot their original sex, and regarded themselves as entirely female. The "soft-men" of the Chukchee Eskimo were ordered into their assumed sex by the elders at childhood, married husbands, and lived as women for the rest of their lives. We hear of Andean sorcerers obliged by tribal custom to change their sexual roles, of Mohave Indian boys publicly initiated into girlhood, of young Tahitians encouraged in infancy to think of themselves as members of the opposite sex. If to modern Westerners the idea of changing sex has seemed, at least until recently, monstrous, absurd, or ungodly, among simpler peoples it has more often been regarded as a process of divine omniscience, a mark of specialness. To stand astride the sexes was not a disgrace but a privilege, and it went often with supernatural powers and priestly functions.

I read of these antique and remote exotica, as you may imagine, with envy and approval, and I read with sympathy too of characters nearer home who found themselves torn between the sexes. There was the poor Abbé de Choisy, a well-known literary cleric and diplomat of eighteenth-century France, who used to receive visitors to his bedroom seductively bedecked in feathers and satins, and who became, as the years wore on, his body thickened, and his face hardened, ever more preposterous. Or there was the celebrated Chevalier d'Éon, who, acquiring a taste for the feminine life during a masquerade in Russia, eventually found himself ordered by his King and Government to live as a woman for the rest of his days—a soldier too, which further endeared him to me, and a person of charming sensibility. Such people probably did not actually believe themselves to *be* women, as I did, or really wish to change their bodies—they merely found it pleasant, convenient, or necessary to act the female role: but still, I felt, as I groped towards their presence in the memoirs and the history footnotes, if they did not actually share my riddle, at least they would have understood it.

The first conformation I found that there were others in the world in precisely my own condition came to me one day in Ludlow, that epitome of the English market town, that picture of castle and parish church, half-timber and boatered butcher. There on a winter evening I espied, reduced to half-price and displayed with a proper obscurity on a high back shelf, a book called *Man Into Woman: An Authentic Record of a Change of Sex.* With what agonies of embarrassment did I edge my way towards that volume! Everything seemed so *wholesome* in that little shop. The cheeks were so rosy, the shoes were so clean, the chat in the corner was about dancing classes, flu, or the shortage of broccoli. *Country Life* and *The Autocar* were the most daring things upon the magazine counter, and I would guess that the bookshelves were dominated by Howard Spring. Good Heavens, I was all wholesomeness myself, still in my British Warm, diffident in the English manner, and fresh as it happened from visiting an old family friend at Richard's Castle. But I steeled myself, sidled alongside, shakily grabbed the volume, and presented it to the saleswoman—who, as I would now foresee, took and wrapped it without a glance, for if there is one thing bookshop assistants decline as a matter of professional principle to take the slightest interest in, it is books.

Man Into Woman told the agonizing story of a young Danish painter, Einar Wegener, who came to think of himself as two people, male and female: not quite like myself, for I believed myself to be one person clad in an alien form, but still a good deal nearer than the poor old powdered Abbé de Choisy, or the cross-sexed wizards of Peru. Haunted and later obsessed by this idea, after years of confusion and misery Wegener found his way, in 1930, to the clinic of a pioneer Dresden sexologist, and there in a series of operations his male physique was stripped from him, and an attempt was made to substitute female organs. They knew nothing of hormones then, and tried to transplant ovaries into his body; but though for a time he was able to live happily enough in his new guise, and abandon altogether his male role, his moment of release was brief. "It is so lovely," he wrote from the women's clinic at Dresden, "to be a woman here among women, to be a female creature exactly like all the others"; but in the very next year he died, and was buried at Dresden as Lili Elbe. There was never a sadder tale. Not only did Wegener lose his health and in the end his life, but after the surgery in the Dresden clinic he never painted another picture until the day he died.

Yet astonishingly, you may think, the story gave me hope. I was not alone. *Please, God, make me a girl,* I had prayed at those innumerable evenings, and I still made the same wish whenever I saw a shooting star, won a wishbone contest, or visited a Blarney Well. Perhaps it could happen yet. With Einar Wegener it failed, with me it might succeed; and even if it meant for me, as it did for him, only a few months or years of fulfillment, would it not be worth it? For I was in my early twenties now, and the older I grew, the more abjectly I realized, when I allowed myself the melancholy thought, that I would rather die young than live a long life of falsehood. A falsehood to whom, you may ask, since I was to all appearances unequivocally a man? A falsehood to me.

I trod the long, well-beaten, expensive, and fruitless path of the Harley Street psychiatrists and sexologists, one after the other, getting their names from their published works, or being passed from one to the other. None of them in those days, I now realize, knew anything about the matter at all, though none of them admitted it. Some palmed me off with avuncular advice. Some gave me blood or urine tests. Some assured me I would grow out of it. One kindly suggested that I join him for a complete analysis, lasting several months—a proposition I wisely declined, for in fact no single soul in my predicament has ever, in the whole history of psychiatry, been "cured" by the science.

I can see that in the state of medical awareness then, it must have been baffling to be confronted by a patently healthy and evidently sane young man declaring himself to be, despite all apparent physical evidence, actually a woman—especially as I did not for a moment wish to be disabused of this belief, only confirmed in it. British psychiatry has traditionally leant towards physical explanations for mental disturbances, only falling back reluctantly upon purely psychological interpretations. But I went a stage further still, and insisted that my own dilemma sprang from sources that neither couch nor drug could isolate, let alone remove. I was insisting that my fantasies were true—that fantasy, in fact, could be a reality in itself. Even now British practitioners seldom seem to grasp the meaning of this idea, and regard the treatment of transsexuals simply as a means of "enabling them to live with their delusions." In those days they were more rigid still, and I can see some of those doctors' faces now, playing helplessly for time and fee as they asked me to describe the symptoms.

Could it not be, they sometimes asked, that I was merely a transvestite, a person who gained a sexual pleasure from wearing the clothes of the opposite sex, and would not a little harmless indulgence in that practice satisfy my, er, somewhat indeterminate compulsions? Alternatively, was I sure that I was not just a suppressed homosexual, like so many others? Nobody would blame me nowadays, surely, if I let my hair down a bit—"wear something a bit gayer, you know, let your *true* personality emerge, don't hide it!" Somebody even arranged a tête-à-tête with a highly civilized homosexual, owner of a London art gallery, whose company it was thought might reconcile me to the condition; we had a difficult lunch together, and he made eyes at the wine waiter over the fruit salad.

But none of it fitted. I did not consider myself a homosexual. I envied women their clothes only as the outward sign of their femininity. The first person I met who really seemed to understand something of the predicament was Dr. Harry Benjamin of New York, to whose clinic in Park Avenue, wearied by the struggle, I eventually found my way. Dr. Benjamin was then in his sixties, I suppose, and looked like a white gnome—white-haired, white-jacketed, white-faced. He seemed too small for his desk, and he talked with a scholarly Viennese accent, like a psychiatrist in a film. "Sit down, sit down—tell me all about yourself. You believe yourself to be a woman? Of course, I perfectly understand. Tell me something about it—take it easy, take it easy—now, tell me, tell me . . ." I told him everything, and it was from him that I learnt what my future would be.

Dr. Benjamin, an endocrinologist, had come later in life

to the study of sexual anxieties, and by the 1950s was deep in the problem of gender confusion. He it was who first formally recognized the existence, within the inner keep of sex, of people like me—people whose problems lay deeper than physical medicine, deeper even than curative psychiatry, and seemed beyond diagnosis or treatment. It was Dr. Benjamin who first called us transsexuals, and to him more than anyone we owe the unveiling of our predicament. In the past twenty years specialists in many countries have applied their minds to the problem, but nobody I think has defined it, let alone resolved it, any more clearly than he did. He had explored every aspect of the condition, and he frankly did not know its cause; what he *did* know was that no true transsexual had yet been persuaded, bullied, drugged, analyzed, shamed, ridiculed, or electrically shocked into an acceptance of his physique. It was an immutable state. "And so I ask myself, in mercy, or in common sense, if we cannot alter the conviction to fit the body, should we not, in certain circumstances, alter the body to fit the conviction?"

Alter the body! Of course this is what I had hoped, prayed, and thrown three-penny bits into wishing wells for all my life; yet to hear it actually suggested, by a man in a white coat in a medical office, seemed to me like a miracle, for the idea of it held for me then, as it holds for me now, a suggestion of sorcery. To alter the body! To expunge those superfluities, like the Phrygians of old, to scour myself of that mistake, to start again, to recapture some of that white freshness I used to feel, singing the psalms at Oxford! To alter the body! To match my sex to my gender at last, and make a whole of me!

I had reached the conclusion myself that sex was not a division but a continuum, that almost nobody was altogether of one sex or another, and that the infinite subtlety of the shading from one extreme to the other was one of the most beautiful of nature's phenomena. Sex was like a biological pointer, but the gauge upon which it flickered was that very different device, gender. If sex was a matter of glands or valves, gender was psychological, cultural, or in my own view spiritual. If one's sex, I reasoned, fell into the right place along the scale of gender, well and good; if it fell anomalously, too far one way or the other, then there came conundrum. But if one could not shift the scale, one could surely move the pointer. Gender might be beyond definition: sex science could understand.

To alter the body! So it really was a possibility for me, as it had been for poor Einar thirty odd years before. A more practical possibility too, for now the sex hormones had been identified, and even without surgery the secondary sexual characteristics could be induced—beards in women, breasts in men, delicacy on the one side, muscles on the other. But a change of the body must be a last resort, Dr. Benjamin counseled me. If it sounded like magic to me, to the world at large it would seem a fearful denouement. Try working out life as a man, he suggested. "Stick it out. Do your best. Try to achieve an equilibrium, that's the best way. Take it easy!" This advice I accepted, for I thought there might be layers to my conundrum which even he could not perceive. Perhaps I depended upon that very clash between sex and gender, so that to tamper with it would be gambling with my very personality? Perhaps it was a condition of my gifts? Perhaps, if as I sometimes thought I was no more than a living parable of the times, to change myself would be to abort the truth—to abort, in a double sense, reality itself? For while I had no doubt at all which was my essential self, I could see that to most people an opposite reality was just as true.

Heavens, I was a jumble, I used wryly to think—two people in one, two truths, the times sublimated, reality aborted! Yet how easily the rest of life seemed to come to me, how fluent if superficial was my pen, how few my mundane worries, so that people used to say I was born with that silver spoon in my mouth, and ask me for advice! My grandfather used to maintain that the essayist E. V. Lucas, a connection of ours, would have been a good writer if he had ever had a care in the world, and some people thought the same of me. In fact I was dark with indecision and anxiety. Sometimes I considered suicide, or to be more accurate, hoped that some unforeseen and painless accident would do it for me, gently wiping the slate clean. And once in desperation I raised with a London doctor the possibility of treatment by female hormones. I thought it might calm my conflicts by feminizing my body to some degree without the finality of surgery—a halfway solution, I thought, better than nothing if less than enough.

A meeting was arranged for me with an endocrinologist in London, and I came home for the appointment from Italy. Since I suppose the event was a fateful one for me, I can remember it with a particular clarity. London was in that heightened version of itself that one always discovers when one returns from abroad—the buses redder than usual, the taxi-drivers more Cockney, and everything more thickly infused with the pungency that is London's own. Even the light that came through the consultancy window was more than reasonably London, much creamier than the Italian light, and charged with the dustflakes of W1. Against it, looking through the window, the gland man stood, and when I entered the room he turned towards me gravely, and rather shyly. He looked, it seems to me, like an Anglo-Indian colonel, tall and gingery and exceptionally clean. He did not sit down. "You do realize," he asked, "what we can and cannot do for you? We can counter your male hormones with female hormones, but we cannot stop their production. We can feminize your body to a considerable extent, but of course the genitals will remain, and there is always the risk of atrophying your male organs. What it would do to your personality or your talent, we cannot say. It is a grave decision to take, but it must be your own. You do know what you are doing?"

I did not, but I went home with a box of estrogen tablets, and for a few nights took one when I went to bed. They left me with a dry taste in the mouth, besides giving me disturbing dreams. I had taken a first timid and tentative step on a long strange path, but I decided after all to obey Dr. Benjamin's advice a little longer, and put the pills away—in my bottom drawer, so to speak, or stored in my heart like Mary's secret (though actually, mistrusting my own resolve, I flushed them down a Venetian lavatory).

intensity with which mature, kind, and cultured men, reading early drafts of this book, looked in it for revelations about the sexual act. Even the most sensitive of my friends, I have come belatedly to realize, in following the course of my life with such kindly concern, have generally been much more interested in my sex than my psyche.

Of course sex interests us all, especially when we are young, and of course there are many men in whose lives it plays no more than a balanced part, just as there are plenty of women obsessed by it. But most men I know find it difficult to distinguish between sex and gender, or even perhaps between sex and self, just as their deepest instincts, however restrained, urge them to polygamy or promiscuousness. Believing as I do *a priori* in the absolute right of anyone to do anything, provided it harms nobody else, I find these sexual addictions entertaining to observe, especially when they are embodied in incongruity. There is something endearingly comic to the spectacle of your English gentleman, for example, forsaking the exquisite pleasures of his home, his adoring wife, his doting children, his books and his pictures, his music and his wines, the inner resources of a magnificent education, the outer assets of a private income, for the apparently still more compelling delights of an evening with a really rather blowsy tart in Paddington! It seems distinctly eccentric behavior to me, but I know from long experience that the gentlest of your male friends, the sweetest of your husbands, is perfectly likely one evening to up and do it.

But for me the actual performance of the sexual act seemed of secondary importance and interest. I suspect this is true for most women, and probably for many men too, but in my case it was half deliberate. I felt that my body was not my own, and encouraged myself in pleasures that were neither penile nor vaginal. Intercourse seemed to me a tool, a reproductive device, and at the same time, in its symbolical fusion of bodies, a kind of pledge or surrender, not to be lightly given, still less thrown away in masquerade. In the ordinary course of events it struck me as slightly distasteful, and I could imagine it only as part of some grand act, a declaration of absolute interdependence, or even a sacrifice. My more immediate physical delights were far more superficial, and much easier to achieve. They were tactile, olfactory, visual, proximate delights—pleasures which, as it happened, I could handily transfer to inanimate objects too, within reason, so that I derived, though I tactfully kept the fact from my more intimate friends, a kindred sensual satisfaction from buildings, landscapes, pictures, wines, and certain sorts of confectionery.

I did not need to ask a barman for these consolations. Throughout my young manhood I was in a constant state of emotional entanglement with somebody or other, sometimes men, sometimes women. Though they gave me pleasure at the time, they were unsatisfactory affairs in the long run, for they were necessarily inconclusive. The men always wanted a girl really, and saw in me I suppose, like Otto in the truck, only a temporary substitute. The girls always wanted a man to cherish them, and soon sensed that I was likely to offer them no more than friendship. And I myself did not quite know what I wanted, or what I might allow myself to want, beyond the touch of the hand or lip, the warmth of the body, the long shared confidences at midnight, the smell of scent or tweed, the laughter and the company. In a sense I was atrophied, but whether by nature or by subconscious volition, I do not know—certainly not from prudery, for if I had been born a woman I fear I might have been rather promiscuous.

"Why, why, why!" screamed an American nympho of my acquaintance, doing her unsuccessful best to seduce me in a hotel bedroom in Athens, but I could not tell her, and if I had she would never have understood. I felt more than ever isolated, neither one thing nor the other, neither seducing nor seducible—only, I flattered myself to think, reasonably seductive.

This was a paradox, and people often sensed it. It was as though I deliberately held myself back from fruition, in work as in pleasure. If sexually I found myself isolated, professionally, as I watched the world go by, I found myself more than ever outside mankind's commitments. More than ever those people down the hill seemed to be pursuing rounds of their own to which I was denied access—not minding their shops now, or sauntering with their holiday amours, but plotting revolutions, fighting elections, conspiring, warring, starving. I was there, by destiny it seemed as by vocation, only and always as an onlooker. An American colleague once described me as "so unobtrusive that one hardly knows he is there at all," while an English critic remarked upon "an odd tendency to disappear as the person behind the style." But it was not modesty that camouflaged me so, nor even professional technique: it was a detachment so involuntary that I often felt that I *really* wasn't there, but was viewing it all from some silent chamber of my own. If I could not be myself, my subconscious seemed to be saying, then I would not be.

SEVEN

RESCUED · A GRAND LOVE · *OBJETS D'ART* · THE NIGHTINGALE

Love rescued me from that remote and eerie capsule, as it rescued me from self-destruction, and everything they say about love, in dicta sublime as in lyric abysmal, is demonstrably true. I have loved people with disconcerting frequency all my life, but I have enjoyed one particular love of an intensity so different from all the rest, on a plane of experience so mysterious, and of a texture so rich, that it overrode from the start all my sexual ambiguities, and acted like a key to the latch of my conundrum.

An exiled Pole once explained to me, in an otherwise empty Cairo restaurant, his conception of infinity. Infinity, he said, was so immense, and its possibilities of coincidence were so illimitable, that somewhere in the universe at that very moment our own conversation was being duplicated, over just the same table, in just such a deserted café, with just such a meal between us. Such a defiance of odds seems to me to govern, very often, the course of true love. Elizabeth, the daughter of a Ceylon tea planter, had been in the Women's Royal Naval Service in the last stages of the war, and had emerged from an unsuccessful engagement to a naval officer to become secretary to Maxwell Ayrton, the architect of Wembley Stadium. She had taken rooms in a house almost opposite Madame Tussaud's. As it miraculously happened I was in London too, taking a brief Arabic course in Bloomsbury, and by a stroke of fortune that stuns me to this day I found myself rooms in that very house (which was kept by a retired brigadier of lascivious tendencies, and his empoodled wife).

Well, I hear you saying, what's so remarkable about that? It is this: that of all the thousands of people who might have lodged in Nottingham Place that summer, the two who found themselves next door to each other two floors up were so instantly, utterly, improbably, and permanently attuned to one another that we might have been brother and sister. People often thought we were, so absolute was our empathy, and we even looked rather alike. She had blue eyes, I had brown, she tanned, I went red, she had a determined organized air, I shambled rather; but we were both thought to have rather a French look to us—she was Huguenot by origin—and as a matter of fact we have always felt particularly at home in France, not by and large a favorite country of the British. Even more than our looks, our manners matched. We did things the same way, and were sensitive to the same nuances. I would not say that there were no secrets at all between us, for every human being, I think, has a right to a locked corner in the mind; but most of our thoughts we shared, and often we need not translate them into words. We were astonishingly *en rapport*. If we were not actually related, it used to be said of us, we had certainly known each other since childhood.

We loved each other's company so much that I often went with her to her office in Hampstead, just for the pleasure of the bus ride, before immediately boarding a bus in the opposite direction to get to my own work halfway across London; and though in the twenty-five years since then we have each had loves of our own, still there remains hardly a moment in my life that I would not rather share with her. She threw a saucepan at me once, and slapped my face in the Windsor train, but still the happiest moments of my existence occur when, coming as we did at our first meeting from opposite ends of the earth, we meet again on the forecourt of Terminal 3, and are exalted again in friendship.

It was a marriage that had no right to work, yet it worked like a dream, living testimony, one might say, to the power of mind over matter—or of love in its purest sense over everything else. People often express themselves baffled by its nature, but it has never seemed strange to me: all the ambivalences of the relationship seem to me petty beside the divine emotion that inspired it. I hid nothing from Elizabeth, explaining to her everything as I had never explained it before: I told her that though each year my every instinct seemed to become more feminine, my entombment within the male physique more terrible to me, still the mechanism of my body was complete and functional, and for what it is worth was hers. For when your lover pants beside you he is not necessarily enjoying the orthodox satisfactions of virility. Fantasies of many sorts are coursing through his mind, multitudinous emotions charge him, perhaps he is raging so not because the life-force is storming from his glands, but because he is dreaming of fire, war, or poetry, or is loving an idea, or loving himself—or *your* self. For my part, in performing the sexual act with Elizabeth I felt I was consummating a trust, and with luck giving ourselves the incomparable gift of children; and she on her side, obeying some mystic alchemy, and disregarding the rivalry of Doge's Palace or *mille feuille*, responded frankly to what I was, and I hope enjoyed herself.

We produced five children, three boys, two girls, but by the nature of things sex was subsidiary in our marriage. In many ways it was a very modern association. It was a friendship and a union of equals, for in our house there could be no dominant male or female place. If we divided our responsibilities, we did it along no lines of sex, but simply according to need or capacity. We hear now of the concept of "open marriage," in which the partners are explicitly free to lead their own separate lives, choose their own friends if they wish, have their own lovers perhaps, restrained only by an agreement of superior affection and common concern. Ours was always such an arrangement. We were never dependent upon each other. For months at a time I would wander off across the world, and sometimes Elizabeth would travel in a different way, into preoccupations that were all her own. Though we were linked in such absences by a rapt concern with each other's happiness, translated frequently, and at vast expense, into transatlantic telephone calls or weekend flights, still we never begrudged each other our separate lives, only finding our mutual affair more exciting when resumed.

The longer we sustained this passionate amity, the less readily I accepted the assurances of marriage counsellors and agony columnists that satisfactory sexual relations were essential to a happy marriage. We could scarcely call our sexual relationship a satisfactory one, since I would have been perfectly content without any sexual relationship at all, yet our lives were full of compensation. Our intimacy was erotic in a different kind, in a sense of arcane and ecstatic understanding, and sometimes a thrust of affection that came not, as it does in romance, like a lullaby or a spring scent, but like a blow between the eyes, a shock to the system, or a suggestion of tragedy—for there must be to all grand loves the perpetual secret dread of an end to it all.

And grand our love has been. It has given nobility to my mostly frivolous life. It has given me always the knowledge of a tremendous possession, like a landowner who travels miserably through foreign countries, rattled in uncomfortable trains, and pestered by confounded aliens, but who remembers now and then the distant calm of his own English acres, with his house serene among its trees in the middle distance, and the leisured sweep of his landscapes all around. I was immensely proud of my marriage. However tangled my inner life, however hateful the mask I wore, if all my ambitions failed and my pen deserted me, still I knew that I had achieved this triumph: a trust that was absolute, and a companionship so endlessly delightful that to this day I would eagerly take that bus to Hampstead each morning, if Elizabeth still worked for Max up there, and I could get a No. 13 back to Aldwych.

But man and wife, only just. It was apparent to Elizabeth sooner than it was to me that I would not be able to soldier on for a lifetime, as the bluffer consultants liked to phrase it, but that one day I must appease my conflicts. Each year my longing to live as a woman grew more urgent, as my male body seemed to grow harder around me. It was like being encased in some preserving substance, another layer added each birthday. I honored, though, an unspoken obligation to our marriage: that until my family was safely in the world, and Elizabeth fulfilled as a mother if not as a wife, I would bide my time. I was afraid that even treatment by hormones, if it did not immediately sterilize me, would have some cruel effect upon children yet to be born; so I waited, intermittently visited some specialist whose contribution to transsexual knowledge I had read about, called on Dr. Benjamin when I was in New York, and settled gradually to the knowledge that here was a problem without absolute solution. I was wonderfully happy in other ways. I did not seem to be mad. Time was still with me.

Meanwhile I watched our family grow. Believer as I could only be in omnisexuality, in the right and ability of humans of every kind to love one another carnally and spiritually, I always respected the emotions of homosexuals; but the truth and pathos of their condition seemed to me exemplified by their childlessness. Years ago I lived briefly in the same house as a devoted homosexual couple, one an eminent pianist, the other a businessman. Their life together was civilized without being in the least chi-chi. Their flat was full of handsome things, their conversation was kind and clever, and when the one was playing I would see the other listening with an expression of truest pride, pleasure, and affection. So real was their bond that when the pianist died the businessman killed himself—and they left behind them, apart from the musician's records, only a void. A marriage as loyal as marriage could be had ended sterile and uncreative; and if the two of them had lived into old age their lives, I think, would have proved progressively more sterile still, the emptiness creeping in, the fullness retreating.

I could not have survived such a life, for my instinct to have children was profound. If I were not a writer, or an artist, I would certainly like to have been a plain mother, for I cannot think of a more fascinating profession than the raising of children, maddening though the little beasts can so often be. Indeed my children and my books, which I was now beginning to write, seemed to me oddly of a kind. With a sad pang I used to watch the aircraft flying overhead, when I had recently delivered a manuscript to my agents, for I imagined that in one of them my book was leaving for America—so long a friend, so quickly mashed into print and book reviews. Conversely my children I regarded rather as works of art. I am ashamed to think I might have loved them less if they had been plain or stupid, and perhaps the truth is that if they *had* been, I would not have known it; they seemed beautiful to me, anyway, slim in physique, nimble in mind, and I watched them developing with the pleasure I might derive from a very well-plotted novel.

Fortunately, though they had their problems like everyone else, they were clearly not the same problems as my own: whatever the causes of my conundrum, they were evidently not hereditary. Nor so far as I could tell did so odd a parentage harm them psychologically. That I was their father in a physical sense was undeniable—they looked very like me, and escaped by the skins of their teeth some of the worse aspects of my temperament. But I was scarcely paternal in any other sense. I was anything but a father-figure, except in that I lived a fairly adventurous life. Nor were my attitudes exactly maternal, either, for even with them I was inhibited by circumstance, my body, and the fear that I might in some way harm them by revealing the truth too soon. Besides, they had a marvelous mother already. No, I stood towards them in my own mind, as in my chemistry, almost as a patron. I had been the instrument of their creation, quite deliberately. I had consciously sparked the fire by which Elizabeth had forged and shaped their being. Like a Medici prince or a proud Elector, though I might sometimes wish that my role in their lives was more direct, that I might pick up a violin now and then to throw off a phrase, or add an afterthought of chiaroscuro with my own brush, still I felt a glow of pride in enabling such lovely objects to exist. There were lesser ways indeed in which they modeled themselves upon me—in turns of phrase, in inessential opinions and prejudices; but the true example of their lives was Elizabeth's, so sure, so all of a piece. I stood, I felt, an impresario in the wings, not always clearly distinguishable, perhaps, in the half-light backstage, but clearly ready to offer a return engagement.

And I hope I made another contribution to the fashioning of those *objets d'art*. I hope I gave them, if nothing else, an understanding of love. It was my specialty. I believed it to be not just a fortuitous abstraction, but a positive energy, even a craft, which could be trained and encouraged. The connotation of love with physical sex seems to me a vulgar simplicism, while the overlapping of the two words I consider one of the weakest points of the English language, bred I suppose out of ancient Bowdlerisms but now obscene in its own right. Love, even unrequited love, even love for inanimates, has given me a sense of possession far more vital than those dim Bonapartist sentiments I felt in childhood. Whole cities are mine, because I have loved them so. So are pictures scattered through the art galleries of the world. If you love something hotly enough, consciously, with care, it becomes yours by symbiosis, irrevocably. I love Wales like this, I love Admiral Lord Fisher (d. 1926), and the greatest pleasure I get from my Abyssinian cat Menelik is the feeling that I have, by the very magnetism of my affection, summoned him from some wild place, some forest or moorland, temporarily to sharpen his claws purring upon my knee.

I loved my children in the same fierce and calculated way, even when they were far away, and I hope they caught the habit in return. Certainly I have received from them always an affectionate if amused attitude of possession. They have looked at me rather as I have looked at Menelik, as some free spirit from somewhere else whom they have enticed and made their own. I have sidled among them, arching my back and trembling my tail, from destinations that must have seemed in their childhood as remote as any Abyssinian heath ("Where *is* Africa, d'you think?" I asked Tom one day, returning from a visit to Sierra Leone. "It is the capital of Paris," he solemnly replied). I must have seemed as different in kind from other children's fathers as Menelik seems, hare-like and tufted, when one sees him consorting with stalwart British tabbies from the farm. But they have known for sure that I was theirs, once and for all in their ownership, and I think they learnt from me, as I learnt from Elizabeth, the colossal constructive force of love, which can bridge chasms and reconcile opposites.

It was not until the eldest boys were in their late teens, they tell me, that they began to realize in what way I was different; for fifteen years at least our marriage looked from the outside not merely successful, but perfectly orthodox, and when I told the first of my friends the unlikely truth about myself, they often thought I was joking.

We lost one child, but even then the desolation of the loss was tempered for me by a sense of continuous possession, and by that streak of perverse optimism I had preserved from my childhood. I felt she would surely come back to us, if not in one guise, then in another—and she very soon did, leaving us sadly as Virginia, returning as Susan, merry as a dancing star. Her first little body is buried beneath a magnolia tree, cherished by sculpted cherubs, outside the door of the Saxon church at Waterperry in Oxfordshire, but her spirit left us, for the time being, on a hot May night in Hampshire.

We had returned from abroad, and had rented half a country house near Newbury. The baby, developing an unidentified virus within two months of her birth, had been taken from us to Newbury hospital, and we knew she was very near death. Elizabeth and I lay sleepless in our room overlooking the garden, too hot and too unhappy even to close our eyes. A great moon shone through the windows, and towards midnight a nightingale began to sing in the tree just outside. I had never heard an English nightingale before, and it was like hearing for the first time a voice from the empyrean. All night long it trilled and soared in the moonlight, infinitely sad, infinitely beautiful, and filling every corner of our room with its resonance. We lay there through it all, each knowing what the other was thinking, the tears running silently down our cheeks, and the bird sang on, part elegy, part comfort, part farewell, until the moon failed and we fell hand in hand into sleep.

In the morning the child had gone.

EIGHT

THREE EMPLOYERS · "ANYBODY FROM THE *GUARDIAN*" · HALF A COLUMN AMONG THE EGYPTIANS · ABHORRENCE

I was a writer. Full as I was of more recondite certainties, I had always been sure of that too. I never for a moment doubted my vocation, except when I briefly pined for a more immediate audience, envying musicians their cadenzas, actors their applause. I spent some ten years in journalism, mostly as a foreign correspondent, and worked for three disparate institutions: the Arab News Agency, in Cairo, *The Times* of London, the *Manchester Guardian.* I would be a hypocrite to pretend I did not enjoy those years. No life could have been more interesting. For a full decade I had a grandstand view of the world's great events, and I was constantly astonished, like Neville Cardus before me, that I was actually being paid for the privilege.

But through it all, unknown certainly to my employers and I assume to my colleagues too, I was tormented by my own ambivalences, and since those were the crucial years of my early thirties, when I was in theory approaching the prime of my manhood, I think it curious to recall my attitudes towards the establishments I worked for—the only three employers, as it happens, that I have had in life.

I was least comfortable with the *Guardian*. This surprises people. If there was one organ in the land which seemed to enshrine the principles generally considered feminine, it was that prodigy of liberalism: pacific, humanist, compassionate, with a motherly eye on underdogs everywhere and a housewifely down-to-earth good sense about everyday affairs. The *Guardian* was kind to nearly everyone, and kindest of all to me, for it let me go more or less where I liked, and seldom cut a word or changed an adjective. Yet I was never at ease with it. There was, I thought, something pallid or drab about its corporate image, something which made me feel exhibitionist and escapist, romantically gallivanting around the world while better men than I were slaving over progressive editorials at home.

I have a disconcerting feeling now that I disliked it because it was like working for a woman rather than a man. I resented the paper's stance of suffering superiority, like a martyred mother of ungrateful children, and did not like being tarred with its earnest, consumer-association, playgroup brush. "Of course we know you're on our side," a young Jordanian dissident once observed to me, pausing from his task of being rude to the British, "because you work for the *Manchester Guardian*," and I squirmed habitually in railway trains, on meeting lifelong and devoted readers of "our paper," to discover just who my audience was. "Anybody from the *Guardian* is a friend of ours," fulsome American voices used to greet me on the doorsteps of academic houses, and the very phrase I came to know as the promise of a ghastly evening. The elements I craved were fire, salt, laughter: the *Guardian*'s specialties were fairness, modesty, and rational assessment. I liked a touch of swank; the *Guardian* shied from it like a horse from a phantom. I was all muddle, conceit, and panache, the *Guardian* all unselfish logic and restraint. I leaned towards the mystic, the *Guardian* had its roots in northern nonconformism, not a faith that appealed to me.

The *Guardian* man who daunted me most was the paper's immensely knowledgeable and universally respected correspondent in Paris. Though I never heard evil spoken of him by a living soul, still we were antipathetic from the start. "How marvelous it must be," I once remarked to him by way of small talk, *apropos* of his great height, "to be able to command every room you enter!" "I do not want," he replied in his most reproving liberal style, "to command anything at all"—an unfortunate response, though he could not know it, to one whose ideals of manhood had been molded by military patterns, and who liked a man to be in charge of things.

Two of my least comfortable memories of the journalistic life concern this disconcerting colleague. The first is the evening when, having at immense pains, by the exertion of his matchless web of contacts, and with an utterly selfless devotion to the task, arranged for me an otherwise totally unobtainable seat on an aircraft into Algiers, then in the first throes of a military rebellion, he discovered that I had missed the flight owing to having dined too long with friends at Maxim's. The second was worse still. On another assignment to North Africa I found myself obliged to dictate a long dispatch home over the telephone *via* Paris; and the only person available to take my message down was the Paris Correspondent himself, the doyen of British observers in

France if not in Europe. My blood froze when I heard it, and one of my notions of Hell remains an eternal dictation of hasty, overromantic, and underinformed dispatches about French colonial affairs to the Paris Correspondent of the *Guardian*. How callow my judgments seemed dropped word by word (he had no shorthand) and often repeated (the line was terrible) into that cold meticulous ear! How shamefully inadequate was my command of the French language, how frivolous my approach to European history, how extravagant were my adjectives—those that, seeing them approaching preposterously purple up my typescript, I did not hastily jettison before they reached me! "Is that all?" he said with a sigh when at last I came to the end of it, and I felt like a blue-nosed comic concluding an engagement booked in awful error in the lecture hall of the Royal Society.

But I must not be ungrateful. The *Guardian* treated me proud, first to last, and though I might not much like the composite *Guardian* reader, still it was invaluable to discover that in every country there were cells of liberals who regarded the paper as holy writ, and who saw in it (as I realized with mixed feelings) all that was best in Britain. After five years with the paper, as a matter of fact, I sometimes began to feel, in moments of especial frailty, symptoms of nonconformist decency, modesty, and restraint within myself.

No such dangers threatened me at *The Times*. *The Times* was very grand in those days, very British, and very masculine. Few women worked for it, none at all in the foreign news departments, and I felt as I had felt in the 9th Lancers the fascination of being a licensed intruder. I never worked for the *Guardian* in England, but I did spend some months at Printing House Square, the home of *The Times* ever since its foundation in 1785, and I remember it less as a newspaper office than as a sort of cabal.

The Times then was a newspaper like no other in the world, an institutionalized anomaly, a national fact of life standing somewhere, perhaps, between the BBC and the Lord Chamberlain's Office, with detectable undertones of the College of Arms (Arundel Herald Extraordinary was actually a member of the staff, and leaving the office in his dignified gray pin-stripe would be seen half an hour later attending some chivalric function dressed up like a playing-card). Even in those last years of the British Empire foreigners still took *The Times* to be an organ of the British Government, and respected—or disrespected—its edicts accordingly. Within Britain people accepted it as the private instrument of a ruling class still cohesive and definable. *The Times* liked to call itself "A Newspaper for Gentlemen, Written by Gentlemen," and the more elderly members of its staff were fluent in snobbish stories about it—"Tell the reporters to wait, Smithers, and show up the gentleman from *The Times*." Though its original reputation had been built upon journalism of the most ferociously competitive kind, by my day it did not consider itself exactly a newspaper at all, but as something entirely and entertainingly *sui generis*—*The Times*, in short.

Printing House Square seemed to me worthy of its tenants. The main part of the office, looking over Queen Victoria Street towards the river, had been designed by a Victorian proprietor of the paper, and built by his own laborers with stone from his own estates. Sir Nikolaus Pevsner considered the best one could read in it was "a certain stodgy staying-power," but I thought it was fine. I used to go to it by tube, and emerging every day from the gloom of Blackfriars Station, I would step into the daylight and see *The Times* there before me like an earnest of permanence—shabby, proud, and self-amused, like postwar London itself, with the Union Jack and its own house flag serene upon its rooftops, and the dowagerlike Rolls-Royce of its editor, leaning slightly upon its rear wheels as it might rest the weight of its buttocks upon a parasol, awaiting orders at the door.

Behind the main block was the eighteenth-century building known as the Private House—a pleasant small town house, appended to the office proper, in which those members of the editorial staff who would now be called "executives" could read their proofs in an armchair, or take their dinner between editions. This was a place that vastly pleased me, in just the same way that men's clubs in London were later to give me an exotic secret satisfaction. There was a butler, I think. There were certainly aproned waitresses. There was a snuffbox with a picture of St. Petersburg upon it. The rooms were leathery and not very well lit, and sometimes eminent guests turned up to dine—politicians, generals, or American columnists who knew everything. I liked the urbane flavor of *The Times*, and I shared its sense of humor.

But if the *Guardian* was too wet for my taste, *The Times* could be too ruthless, and the episode that most affected me at Printing House Square was an affair of sensibilities. I was being groomed for a foreign correspondent's job, and part of my apprenticeship was to serve as an assistant to the Foreign News Editor, Ralph Deakin. Deakin was already a folk-figure of Printing House Square, having been there since the world began, and it was he who, in his customary address of welcome to new recruits, habitually quoted the example of

Frank Riley, a young and brilliant reporter, an Oxford man too, who had been murdered by the soldiers of Feng Yu-hsiang at Chengchow in 1927—"but," as Deakin used to say with proud solemnity, "he had his just reward—half a column of obituary in *The Times*, and he was still in his thirties."

Deakin was aging, and the progress of *The Times*, though I would hardly call it headlong, was fast leaving him behind. Week by week I noticed not merely a faltering in the old gentleman himself, but a progressive disregard of his views. People did not listen to him. Decisions were taken without his knowledge. He clearly sensed it too, and was distressed. For what seem to have been hours at a time, talking in an infinitely slow grating voice that was, I admit, among the heavier of my burdens, he would disclose to me his anxieties or more often his resentments—for he was not rich in the milk of human kindness himself, and could be malicious. I did my best to cheer him up, for I was very sorry for him, but it was becoming apparent to both of us that he was losing place, and the last straw came when, well before his due time for retirement, he was asked to go.

The consequences had a profound and permanent effect upon me, and helped to sour me, I think now, against such close-knit societies of male traditionalism. I know only Deakin's side of the dispute, but he told me that after forty years of almost fanatical service to the paper, he had been told to leave almost at once. He had begged them, he told me, to allow him to sit out the last few months, or perhaps, following an old *Times* precedent, to appoint him to some comfortable sinecure, like a correspondentship in Switzerland.

But they refused him everything, he said. He grew increasingly talkative, bitter, and confused, our *tête-à-têtes* lasted longer every day, and finally, one evening in the winter of 1952, he gave me a letter. If anything should happen to him, he said, buttoning his thick black overcoat, straightening his Homburg, and removing his walking stick from its stand behind the desk, I was to give it to the higher authorities of *The Times*; and gently chewing—for he generally seemed to have in his mouth, when not a cigar, some kind of lubricant lozenge, perhaps to keep his voice going—he nodded at me in his usual way, said good night with his habitual icy trace of a smile, and went home to kill himself with sleeping pills.

What was I to do? I had thought of refusing the letter, but sensed that I was almost the only confidant he had in the world, and hadn't the heart. I had tried in my ineffectual way to sustain him—but denied as I was my instinctive impulse to take the poor old man in my arms and cherish him, I failed I fear to show him how much I cared, and I am sorry for it to this day. The foreign editor, seeing me later that evening, sensed that I had undergone some cruel experience: "You look as though you've seen a ghost," he said, and perhaps with his Scottish vision he was right. *The Times,* however, rose easily above its remorse. When the news of Deakin's death reached the office next day, I duly handed in the letter; but it was never mentioned at the inquest, which was reported at length in the *Daily Telegraph,* but scarcely at all in our own columns.

The verdict was, as *The Times* doubtless wished it, one of accidental death; but after all, Ralph Deakin did get fourteen column inches of obituary.

No, the job that really suited me best was the one with the Arab News Agency, for that curious organization really had no corporate image at all, but was a loose confederation of mavericks. I came to it impetuously. Leaving the Army, and finding myself with a year to spare before Oxford could have me back, I conceived the idea of Doing Something for the Arabs, for whose cause in Palestine I had developed an earnest sympathy. I looked up the word "Arab" in the London telephone book, and discovered there the address of this promising concern, which seemed to offer me the dual chance of a journalistic experience and a worthy cause. I rang them up at once, and presently they sent me to Cairo.

I had first seen the coast of Egypt in the company of Otto, approaching Port Said late at night on our troopship from Italy, and as we sailed towards the distant lights he had said to me, "Ah! Do you smell it? That's the smell of Egypt! That's n-n-nectar!" The very source of that smell, or its vortex, was the Immobilia Building in Sharia Sherif Pasha, Cairo, where the Arab News Agency had its head office. There it was overpowering. Its basis was, I now think, inadequately refined petrol, but to this foundation were added many subtle extras: dust, of course, and dirt, and animals, and a touch of jasmine, that rose of Egypt, and grilled mutton, and cooking oil, and new concrete, and laid upon it all like grated cheese upon a rich soup, the sealing smell of sunshine.

Groping through this fragrance, all around the Immobilia Building, were the noises of Cairo, which in those days were a harsh blend of the modern and the medieval. The cars hooted, the buses roared, the trams clanked overloaded around their precarious loops, but one heard too the cries of the street peddlers, musically echoing in the side streets, and the resonant call of the muezzin, not yet coarsened by electronics, the clopping of donkeys and the flip-flop of camels, and even sometimes the gentle chanting of the blind sages still employed by rich men, in that long-discredited Egypt, perpetually to recite the Koran at their doorsteps.

In the very middle of it all, topographically as politically, worked the journalists of the Arab News Agency, up on the first floor. Our job was to collect news from all over the Arab world, and then to disseminate it among Arabic newspapers, radio stations, and magazines from Syria to South Arabia. The agency was British-owned, and employed a handful of Britons in its Cairo office, but it liked to keep up Arab appearances, for discretion's sake, and did everything bilingually.

I was happy there. The rank-and-file Britons with the agency were in effect poor whites. We were honorary Levantines. Our motives for being there were distinctly mixed, and while some of us had come out from England just for the interest of the job, others had gravitated there through complex permutations of war, love, and error, and had Greek wives at Heliopolis, or undisclosed commitments in Bulaq. For myself I lived chiefly in a no man's land between expatriate and indigene. My friends were mostly in the office, some Egyptian, some British, and we were none of us rich. We were boulevardiers, but of a modest rank, frequenting the shabbier of the downtown pavement cafés, where the lesser Egyptian bourgeoisie played interminable games of dominoes, or laboriously mouthed to themselves the headlines of *Al Ahram*—shabby places with marble-topped tables and dirty glass partitions, where the coffee was as thick as porridge, and the water tumblers were a perpetual dingy gray. There we would sit and talk in the early evening, when the long siesta was nearly over, and a momentary stillness lay on the capital, until we heard the rattle of the heavy steel shutters being raised one by one from the shopfronts, and it was time for us to saunter back to Immobilia, climb the wide, dark, pompous steps to the first floor, and start work on the evening bulletin.

This was never boring. The news was full of drama. The war in Palestine was at its height, affairs within Egypt were rich in intrigue, menace, and corruption, and our correspondents in the remoter Arab parts flooded us with piquant intelligence—marvelous cameos of desert crime, court conspiracy, religious polemic, or family feud. Besides, we did our work in a spirit of Bohemian release. Occasionally, it is true, the noise of a riot outside, or the scream of the sirens that marked the passage of King Farouk towards the Mohammed Ali Club, brought the realities of Cairo more than professionally close; but generally, once we were inside our dim-lit, crowded, and untidy rooms, we would forget the truth about ourselves, forget the shabby villa off the airport road, forget the impending misery of the midnight tram, forget the scuffed shoes and the stained tarboosh, forget the swarming children and the skinny black-veiled wife, forget our lost hopes of a career in the law, or the Ministry of the Interior, forget that we were indigent Egyptian effendim or struggling Levantines, forget even our sexual ambiguities, and lose ourselves in that strange little world of our own upstairs.

It is oddly true that there in the heart of Muslim Cairo, women were more naturally accepted in the office than they would have been at the *Guardian,* let alone Printing House Square. The girl telephone operators shared the simple office jokes as easily and agreeably as they shared the roast pigeon, brought in by the office boy wrapped in copy paper from the street stalls outside; and as for me, I sensed in Cairo for the first time a curious acceptance or absorption which was to bind me for many years to the Muslim countries of the East, and play, when the time came, a decisive part in my small destiny.

Such were my only employers. By the time I resigned from the last of them, in 1961, I felt myself to be so isolated in my quandary that I could not bear to work in company or at behest, and set off on my own path professionally as I had so long trodden it in my private life; for by then I found the figure I cut in the world, however innocuous it seemed to others, abhorrent to myself.

NINE

TO EVEREST · THE MALE BRILLIANCE THE MALE RHYTHM · A HOLY MAN

So far it was abhorrent chiefly in the idea of it. Though I resented my body, I did not dislike it. I rather admired it, as it happened. It might not be the body beautiful, but it was lean and sinewy, never ran to fat, and worked like a machine of quality, responding exuberantly to a touch of the throttle or a long haul home. Women, I think, never have quite this feeling about their bodies, and I shall never have it again. It is a male prerogative, and contributes no doubt to the male arrogance. In those days, though for that very reason I did not want it, still I recognized the merits of my physique, and had pleasure from its exercise.

I first felt its full power, as one might realize for the first time the potential of a run-in car, in 1953, when I was assigned by *The Times* to join the British expedition shortly to make the first ascent of Mount Everest. This was essentially a physical undertaking. The paper had exclusive rights to dispatches from the mountain, and I was to be the only correspondent with the team, my job being partly to see that dispatches from the expedition's leader got safely home to London, but chiefly to write dispatches of my own. The competition would be intense and very likely violent, communications were primitive to a degree, and the only way to do the job was to climb fairly high up the mountain myself and periodically, to put a complex operation simply, run down it again with the news. It was not particularly to my credit that I was given the assignment—at an agile twenty-six I was patently better suited for it than most of my colleagues at Printing House Square. I took exercise daily (as I still do), did not smoke (and still don't), and though excessively fond of wine, seldom drank spirits, not much liking the taste of them.

I was also, being some years out of the 9th Lancers, furiously keen. There is something about the newspaper life, however specious its values and ridiculous its antics, that brings out the zest in its practitioners. It may be nonsense, but it is undeniably fun. I was not especially anxious to achieve fame in the trade, for I already felt instinctively that it would not be my life's occupation, but even so I would have stooped to almost any skulduggery to achieve what was, self-consciously even then, quaintly called a scoop. The news from Everest was to be mine, and anyone who tried to steal it from me should look out for trouble.

In such a mood, at such an age, at the peak of a young man's physical condition, I found myself in May, 1953, high on the flank of the world's greatest mountain.

Let me try to describe the sensation for my readers, as it seems to me today—and especially for my women readers, who are unlikely I now see to have experienced such a conjunction of energies.

Imagine first the setting. This is theatrically changeable. In the morning it is like living, reduced to minuscule proportions, in a bowl of broken ice cubes in a sunny garden. Somewhere over the rim, one assumes, there are green trees, fields and flowers; within the bowl everything is a brilliant white and blue. It is silent in there. The mountain walls deaden everything and cushion the hours in a disciplinary hush. The only noise is a drip of water sometimes, the howl of a falling boulder or the rumble of a distant avalanche. The sky above is a savage blue, the sun glares mercilessly off the snow and ice, blistering one's lips, dazzling one's eyes, and filling that mountain declivity with its substance.

In the afternoon everything changes. Then the sky scowls down, high snow-clouds billow in from Tibet, a restless cruel wind blows up, and before long the snow is falling in slanted parallel across the landscape, blotting out sky, ridges, and all, and making you feel that your ice-bowl has been put back into the refrigerator. It is terribly cold. The afternoon is filled with sounds, the rush of wind, the flapping of tent-canvas, the squeak and creak of guy-ropes; and as the evening draws on the snow piles up around your tent, half burying it infinitesimally in the hulk of Everest, as though you have been prematurely incarcerated, or perhaps trapped in a sunken submarine—for you can see the line of snow slowly rising through the nylon walls of the tent, like water rising to submerge you.

But imagine now the young man's condition. First, he is constant against this inconstant background. His body is running not in gusts and squalls, but at a steady high speed. He actually tingles with strength and energy, as though sparks might fly from his skin in the dark. Nothing sags in him. His body has no spare weight upon it, only muscles made supple by exercise. When, in the bright Himalayan morning, he emerges from his tent to make the long trek down the mountain to the Khumbu glacier below, it is as though he could leap down there in gigantic strides, singing as he goes. And when, the same evening perhaps, he labors up again through the driving snow, it is not a misery but a challenge to him, something to be outfaced, something actually to be enjoyed, as the deep snow drags at his feet, the water trickles down the back of his neck, and his face thickens with cold, ice, and wind.

There is no hardship to it, for it is not imposed upon him. He is the master. He feels that anything is possible to him, and that his relative position to events will always remain the same. He does not have to wonder what his form will be tomorrow, for it will be the same as it is today. His mind, like his body, is tuned to the job, and will not splutter or falter. It is this feeling of unfluctuating control, I think, that women cannot share, and it springs of course not from the intellect or the personality, nor even so much from upbringing, but specifically from the body. The male body may be ungenerous, even uncreative in the deepest kind, but when it is working properly it is a marvelous thing to inhabit. I admit it in retrospect more than I did at the time, and I look back to those moments of supreme male fitness as one remembers champagne or a morning swim. Nothing could beat me, I knew for sure; and nothing did.

I think for sheer exuberance the best day of my life was my last on Everest. The mountain had been climbed, and I had already begun my race down the glacier towards Katmandu, leaving the expedition to pack its gear behind me. By a combination of cunning and ingenuity I had already sent a coded message through an Indian Army radio transmitter at Namche Bazar, twenty miles south of Everest, its operators being unaware of its meaning; but I did not know if it had reached London safely, so I was myself hastening back to Katmandu and the cable office with my own final dispatch. How brilliant I felt, as with a couple of Sherpa porters I bounded down the glacial moraine towards the green below! I was brilliant with the success of my friends on the mountain, I was brilliant with my knowledge of the event, brilliant with muscular tautness, brilliant with conceit, brilliant with awareness of the subterfuge, amounting very nearly to dishonesty, by which I hoped to have deceived my competitors and scooped the world. All those weeks at high altitude had suited me, too, and had given me a kind of heightened fervor, as though my brain had been quickened by drugs to keep pace with my body. I laughed and sang all the way down the glacier, and when next morning I heard from the radio that my news had reached London providentially on the eve of Queen Elizabeth's coronation, I felt as though I had been crowned myself.

I never mind the swagger of young men. It is their right to swank, and I know the sensation!

Once more on Everest I was the outsider—formally this time, as well as tacitly. None of the climbers would have guessed, I am sure, how irrevocably distinct I felt from them; but they were aware that I was not a climber, and had been attached to the expedition only to watch. At first I was supposed to provide my own victuals and equipment, but it seemed rather silly to maintain such segregation twenty thousand feet above nowhere, so I soon pooled my resources with theirs, and pitched my tent among them.

On Everest, nevertheless, I realized more explicitly some truths about myself. Though I was as fit as most of those men, I responded to different drives. I would have suffered almost anything to get those dispatches safely back to London, but I did not share the mountaineers' burning urge to see that mountain climbed. Perhaps it was too abstract an objective for me—certainly I was not animated by any respect for inviolate nature, which I have always disliked, preferring like George Leigh-Mallory a blend of tame and wild. I was pleased when they did climb Everest, but chiefly for a less than elevated reason—patriotic pride, which I knew to be unworthy of their efforts, but which I could not suppress.

I well understood the masochistic relish of challenge which impelled them, and which stimulated me too, but the blankness of the achievement depressed me. One of the older Everesters, H. W. Tilman, once quoted G. K. Chesterton to illustrate the urge of alpinism: "I think the immense act has something about it human and excusable; and when I endeavor to analyze the reason of this feeling I find it to lie, not in the fact that the thing was big or bold or successful, but in the fact that the thing was perfectly useless to everybody, including the person who did it." Leigh-Mallory presumably meant much the same, when he talked of climbing Everest simply "because it was there." But this elusive prize, this snatching at air, this nothingness, left me dissatisfied, as I think it would leave most women. Nothing had been discovered, nothing made, nothing improved.

I have always discounted the beauty of clouds, because their airy impermanence seems to me to disqualify them from the truest beauty, just as I have never responded to kinetic art, and love the shifting light of nature only because it reveals new shapes and meanings in the solids down below. Nor do I like sea views, unless there is land to be seen beyond them. A similar distrust of the ephemeral or the un-finite weakened my response to the triumph of Everest in 1953. It was a grand adventure, I knew, and my part in relaying its excitements to the world was to transform my professional life, and dog me ever after; yet even now I dislike that emptiness at its climax, that perfect uselessness, and feel in a slightly ashamed and ungrateful way that it was really all rather absurd.

For it was almost like a military expedition—the colonel in command, not so long from Montgomery's staff, the little army of porters who wound their way bent-back with their loads over the hills from Katmandu, the meticulously packed and listed stores, the briefings, the air of ordered determination. It was a superbly successful expedition—nobody killed, nobody disgraced—and looking back upon it now I see its cohesion as a specifically male accomplishment. Again constancy was the key. Men more than women respond to the team spirit, and this is partly because, if they are of an age, of a kind, and in a similar condition, they work together far more like a mechanism. Elations and despondencies are not so likely to distract them. Since their pace is more regular, all can more easily keep to it. They are distinctly more rhythm than melody.

In 1953 the rhythm was steadier than it might be now, for it was conscious then as well as constitutional. Stiff upper lip and fair play were integral to the British masculine ethos, and shame was a powerful impulse towards achievement. Social empathy, too, strongly reinforced the sense of maleness. The functional efficiency of class I had already discovered in the Army, and it was the same on Everest. Hunt's climbers were men of the officer class, as they would then have been called, and they were bound by common tastes and values. They spoke the same language, shared the same kind of past, enjoyed the same pleasures. Three of them had been to the same school. In a social sense they formed a kind of club; in an imperial sense, and this was almost the last of the imperial adventures, they were a company of sahibs attended by their multitudinous servants.

One could not, I think, apply these categories to women of equal intelligence in similar circumstances, and less and less can one now apply them to men. Class has lost its binding function; patriotism has lost its elevating force; young men are no longer ashamed of weaknesses; the stiff upper lip is no longer an ideal, only a music hall sally. The barrier between the genders is flimsier now, and no expedition will ever again go to the Himalayas so thoroughly masculine as Hunt's. It embarrasses me rather to have to admit that from that day to this, none has gone there more successfully.

I need not belabor my sense of alienation from this formidable team. I liked most of its members very much, and have remained friends with some to this day, but my sense of detachment was extreme, and though I shamelessly accepted their help throughout the adventure, still I was always at pains to cherish my separateness. I hated to think of myself as one of them, and when in England we were asked to sign menus, maps, or autograph books, I used carefully to sign myself James Morris of *The Times*—until the climbers, fancying I fear altogether different motives in me, asked me not to. At the same time a wayward self-consciousness—for I was a child of the age, too—compelled me to keep up male appearances, perhaps as much for my own persuasion as for anyone else's. I even overdid it rather. I grew a beard, and when at the end of the expedition I walked into the communications room at the British Embassy in Katmandu with my tin mug jangling from the belt of my trousers, the wireless operator asked acidly if I *had* to look so jungly. He did not know how cruelly the gibe hurt, for in a few words it cut this way and that through several skins of self-protection.

Everest taught me new meanings of maleness, and emphasized once more my own inner dichotomy. Yet paradoxically my most evocative memory of the experience haunts me with a truth of an altogether different kind. Often when there was a lull on the mountain I would go down the glacier and wander among the moraines. Sometimes I went south, towards the distant Buddhist temple at Thyangboche where the deodars shaded the green turf, and the bells, gongs, and trumpets of the monks sounded from their shambled refectory. Sometimes I clambered into the snows of the north, towards the great wall of the Lho La, over whose ominous white ridge stood the peaks of Tibet. I vaguely hoped to catch a glimpse of an abominable snowman, and I was looking too for traces of the lemurs and mountain hares which sometimes, I had been told, penetrated those high deserts.

I saw no animals ever. What I found instead was a man. I saw him first in the extreme distance, across an absolutely blank snowfield at about nineteen thousand feet, to which I had climbed from the glacier below for the sake of the view. At first I was frightened, for I could not make out what he was—only a small black swaying speck, indescribably alone in the desolation. As he came closer I saw that he could only be human, so I plunged through the loose snow to meet him, and presently, there near the top of the world, thousands of feet and many miles above the trees, the streams, or human habitation, we met face to face. It was the strangest encounter of my life.

He was a holy man, wandering in the mountains, I suppose, for wandering's sake. His brown, crinkled, squashed-up face looked back at me expressionless from beneath a yellow

TEN

A TRACE OF PARANOIA? · A BAD WORLD · NO PLACE FOR ME

By my mid-thirties my self-repugnance was more specific, and more bitter, and I began to detest the body that had served me so loyally. After the conception of Virginia I began another tentative experiment with hormones, thinking that some degree of feminization might weaken the intensity of my distress, and allow me to stagger on through life without any more drastic denouement. When the child died, though, I abandoned this attempt, and watched myself helpless and repelled as I advanced towards a male middle age. This was the worst period of my life. I did not know what best to do, I was tormented by an ever increasing sense of isolation from the world and from myself, and I was plunged into periods of despair that frightened Elizabeth and debilitated me. I began to suffer migraines, of the classic kind—distortions of vision and of speech which were preceded by periods of terrific elation, as though I had been injected with some gloriously stimulating drug, but which worked themselves out miserably in shattering headaches.

Now for the first time, perhaps, my anxieties developed into a trace of paranoia. I loathed not merely the notion of my maleness, and the evidence of my manhood. I resented my very connection with the male sex, and hated to be thought, even by my dearest friends, a member of it. Since I still looked to all appearances very much a man, this meant that all day long I was jarred by reminders of my condition, or infuriated by well-meant pleasantries—"You won't be interested in this, this is women's talk," or "*What* fun for Joanna, to have a young man around the house!" At formal dinner parties, usually among diplomats, I grew to dread the moment when the ladies left the dinner table, leaving me squirming and alone with the port, the cigars, and the awful possibility of after-dinner stories. Almost my only moments of relief occurred when, now as always, sensitive souls recognized the feminine in me, and made me feel they understood; or better still, when in my dreams I was released from my conflicts altogether, and seemed to look down upon my unhappiness as from a great distance, dressed in air—

Only in sleep
did the ice melt
from about him
and then he would
                    fly
                    low
and to any distance
                    over the oceans

My quandary was becoming obsessive, however hard I tried to concentrate upon my work, however comforting the consolations of family and friendship. The strain was telling on me—not only the strain of playing a part, but the strain too of living in a male world. This had been fun enough at first, among the indulgent elegance of the 9th Lancers, but in a muddled and unhealthy way I had come to hate it. I had been for ten years a busy foreign correspondent, and if no life could be more enthralling, equally no life could be more full of disillusionment. No foreign correspondent of my acquaintance has been either a snob or a sycophant, but few have been optimists, either. They have seen the worst too soon in life, and they know the frauds of fame and power.

For myself, I suppose, I instinctively associated those deceits with the male condition, since then even more than now the world of affairs was dominated by men. It was like stepping from cheap theater into reality, to pass from the ludicrous goings-on of minister's office or ambassador's study into the private house behind, where women were to be found doing real things, like bringing up children, painting pictures, or writing home; and though I know this is a footling simplicism, and that realities all too terrible hang upon the labors of public men, still I began to feel that the private part of any life was the only part that mattered. Men, when they turned from their trade to their hobby, became less aggressively men. It was in the great world outside that their grosser and sillier instincts found expression; at home, as the gossip writers well understood, they could be almost human.

And what a world it was, through which I wandered increasingly confused down the 1950s and 1960s! I reported little but misery or chicanery, as I flew from war to rebellion, famine to earthquake, diplomatic squabble to political trial. I listened to the pratings of corrupt politicians, or the bombast of stupid generals. I investigated reports of torture, false imprisonment, intimidation. I watched the mock-marriages of tinsel monarchs, anxious only to perpetuate their dynasties. I saw people bombed, and rocketed, and beaten, and evicted. I met Che Guevara sharp as a cat in Cuba, and Guy Burgess swollen with drink and self-reproach in Moscow, and Kim Philby, whom I thought I could have loved, deceiving us all in Lebanon. I watched Eichmann humdrum and offended within the bullet-proof glass of his courtroom cage, the common man personified as the murderer he was. I saw Powers the aerial spy paraded before the People's Court, the peasants stumbling in to give their evidence like figures from Tolstoy, the thick-set judges solemn at their dais, the sense of vast unseen forces at play behind those puppets. I watched my own beloved Army floundering in degradation as it was forced, year by year, from its last imperial footholds, now and then spitting back like a cornered animal, and forced at last into that distasteful ignominy, Suez.

Everywhere I met unhappy pawns of oppression, or at least of circumstance: brilliant unhappy writers in Poland, gristly black leaders in the American South, frustrated churchmen in Rhodesia, people who wanted me to smuggle letters out of Leningrad or currency into Prague, and everywhere in those days the young patriots, passionate in their love of race or country, who thought they saw in political liberation the answer to the world's sorrows. I saw the dismembered bodies of politicians in Iraq; I saw the charred victims of napalm in Sinai; I knew too well the frenzied mouthing and posturing of the mob, anywhere in the world, when it had a cause to kill or burn for, or a charismatic leader to inspire it. Philby once quoted to me a passage of my own, in which I had tried to express my feelings about the British action at Suez, when our allies in aggression had been the Israelis and the French. There was, I had written, "a despairing, pitiful dignity to the part the British played in that forlorn campaign, as of a thoroughbred gone wild among mustangs." Philby thought this sentence comic. "Despairing, pitiful dignity! Thoroughbred gone wild!" He laughed at it, but without humor, and even then, though I was privy to none of his secrets, I knew what he was thinking. He was thinking that there was no true dignity in the world of affairs, no thoroughbred integrity, no pity either. It was all rotten. It was all lies. There was no place in it for innocent surmise.

No place for me, either. You must not think me conceited if I claim that, for some years in my thirties and forties, I had a world at my feet. My work was well known on both sides of the Atlantic, and the opportunities I was offered were almost unbounded. In newspapers, in television, in politics, even in diplomacy I have no doubt that I could have made for myself a long and successful career. I was exceedingly confident of my abilities, and this gave confidence to others too, and opened many doors for me.

But I wanted none of it. It was repugnant to me. I thought of public success itself, I suppose, as part of maleness, and I deliberately turned my back on it, as I set my face against manhood. I resigned from my last job, withdrew from the chances of public life, and took to writing books, or traveling in my own behalf. I was cultivating impotence.

ELEVEN

PLEASING MY SENSES · THE LUST OF VENICE · THE SOLACE OF AFRICA SUBLIMATIONS

For if I had no wish to be an activist in public affairs, nor did I want sexual potency. I wanted to be rid of it. One has only to remember the lengths to which elderly Arab gentlemen allegedly go to maintain their virility, smoking the skins of lizards or eating the powdered horns of rhinoceroses, to realize how startling this ambition would be to most men. I did not think of impotence, however, as lack of passion. I had never considered the act of intercourse the best part of sex, but I made up for this lack of spermal enthusiasm, I think, in the variety of my sensual satisfactions. They were truly erotic pleasures I derived from the lush and languid hours of those Oxford afternoons; and I do not doubt that the elaboration of my prose, too, which all too often declined into rhetoric, but did have its moments of splendor, owed much to what I was.

As it happens many of the artists I most admire, or feel most akin to, seem to have led limited or frustrated sexual lives, channeling their personality into their work instead, or perhaps taming it there. I think for instance of Emily Eden, the witty spinster chronicler of life in Anglo-India, of Jane

Austen, of the impotent Ruskin; of the childless Disraeli with his elderly bride, of Harold Nicolson and his adored bisexual Vita, of Turner and Mendelssohn, of the voluptuary Flecker and the confused T. E. Lawrence. I remember my dear Kinglake, bachelor champion of women's rights, of whom a woman obituarist wrote: "His book *Eothen* will live forever . . . but he himself, that marvelous mixture of pride, of humility, of daring and intense shyness, of affection and cynicism, will never be known."

Robert Stoller, an American psychiatrist who has made a study of transsexuality in children, has written of the patients he has analyzed: "The artistic interests of these little boys are those our Western society considers more feminine than masculine, for while these boys are intelligent, active, curious, and original, their creativity is sensual, not intellectual. They touch, stroke, smell, hear, look, and taste—they create to please their senses." Creating to please my senses was certainly my own literary method, which accounts perhaps for a striking inaccuracy in the use of dates, and a lifelong inability to master the points of the compass. I was necessarily secretive in my feelings, and many of my emotions I expended upon works of art, gifts of nature, and above all places.

Bear with me, then, poised as my narrative is on the brink of denouement, while I describe the influence upon me of two places in particular. They meant much to me, and never more than in those last years of ambivalence—for the more distracted I was, the more obsessively I traveled.

The first is Venice. This is one of the cities I own, because I have written a book about it, but it is also a city in which I am always the foreigner. I have little in common with the

Venetians; few of their instincts are mine; I move through their city as through some marvelous exhibition, bemused by its beauty and intrigued by its inhabitants, but never for a moment feeling indigenous.

I first lived in Venice at the end of the Second World War, when I was temporarily detached from regimental duties to help organize the motorboats of the place. All the best of these had been commandeered by the British Army, and our job was to see that they were properly used by the military, and that the generals and staff officers who arrived with suspicious frequency on official visits to the city were conveyed in proper style up the Grand Canal. The work was light. The spell of the place was intoxicating. Very soon I felt Venice to be mine, and I can remember still the proprietorial pleasure with which, ushering another batch of bigwigs into one of the posher boats, I took them off for their first glimpse of the Serenissima—even the sternest faces among them softening as wonder succeeded wonder, light dappled against light, and even the haughtiest deigning to respond to my glow of delight with a detectable if guarded smile.

Of those who have written books in English about Venice, none I think have had such an introduction to the city as mine. Venice was half deserted, half dead perhaps. There were no tourists at all. The war had left the place unscathed but melancholy, and it lay there silent and abandoned in its lagoon, clothed always (it seems to me in memory) in a pale green light, and echoing with footfalls. Most of the people I worked with were Venetians, and they would tell me often of the splendors of the place before the war, brilliant always, they assured me, with patricians and film stars, galas and displays. But I loved it as it was, and the mingled strain of pathos and wistfulness that pervaded the city then has colored my view of it always, and has left me, now that very different sensations charge it, at last disenchanted with the place.

The exuberance of Venice I learnt much later, when Elizabeth and I had our own flat on the Grand Canal, in the little red palace that forms the corner of the Rio San Trovaso. We were supported by publishers and magazine editors, possessed a boat and two merry children, and lived up there in a condition of more or less constant ecstasy. We had a year in Venice *en famille*, and experienced its long winter malaise and its blistering summer, as well as its Elysian spring; but we did not care about the seasons, for we made our own weather, and sailed the lagoon in our little leaky boat as bold as in-shore Tritons.

Boldest of all at night, for sometimes after dinner, especially if friends from home were with us, reckless and laughing with wine we would creep down the stairs of the old palace, braving the chinks of light which, surreptitiously revealed from chained door or curtained window, testified to the unremitting interest of our neighbors; and unfastening the boat from its mooring in the side-canal, with difficulty we would start up its engine and sail down the Grand Canal, past the great bulk of the Salute until, as though we were passing into some undiscovered country, we entered the wide lagoon. I know of no more marvelous sensation than to be afloat in the Venetian lagoon slightly drunk with friends in the middle of a summer night. The water then seems viscous and inky. The smell is a heady compound of mud, salt, and sewage. A distant hiss and roar marks the presence of the open sea beyond the Lido. And away to the west (I think) Venice creamily rides the darkness, all light and fancy, the pale shapes of its buildings moving one against the other in thrilling perspective. The spectacle used to strike me speechless with pleasure, and handing the tiller to somebody else, I would lie in the bows of the boat, trailing my fingers in the muddy water, submitting to what I still think to have been the most truly libidinous of a lifetime's varied indulgences—the lust of Venice.

For long after we left the city I contrived to go back there most years, and Venice played a telling part, emotional and suggestive as well as professional, in the development of my life. Like Oxford, Venice was always feminine to me, and I saw her perhaps as a kind of ossification of the female principle—a stone equivalent, in her grace, serenity, and sparkle, of all that I would like to be. There used in those days to be a blind beggar woman generally on the steps of the Accademia bridge, on the gallery side. She sat on the ground with her back to the bridge parapet, her knees hunched up beneath their serge skirts, holding out her hand for charity. I looked forward to seeing this lady whenever I returned to Venice, and generally gave her something as I passed towards San Marco, but once I went further, and slipping her the usual few lire, I squeezed her hand as well. A miracle then happened. She squeezed mine in return, and in the pressure of her old fingers I knew for certain that she understood me in her blindness, and was responding woman to woman.

I came much later to the sympathy of Africa. I had disliked the continent always, except for those regions which had been illuminated by the light of Islam. I loathed the fetishes, the meaningless high jinks, the edible slugs, the tribal savageries, the arrogant upstart politicians, the ludicrous epauletted generals, the frightening art, the empty history (for I am skeptical even now about those lost civilizations of the African past). Black Africa seemed everything I wanted *not* to be, from the hearty to the vicious, by way of the stuck-up. I found the black African as incomprehensible as a man from the moon—certainly far more alien to me than my cat or my sheepdog Sam—and while I knew intellectually that black people were as diverse as white, that there were good and bad Africans, wise and foolish, that they bled or wept like Jews or Welshmen, yet emotionally I viewed them as one people, and did not trust their values.

But quite late in travel, when my own reactions were changing and my sensibilities had become more flexible, I came abruptly to see the black Africans in different terms altogether. I learnt to accept them not at my values at all, but at theirs. I was a child of the imperial times, and this was a difficult process, akin I think to the trouble old-fashioned parents have in adjusting to premarital relations, or one's own baffled efforts to appreciate electronic music. It meant starting afresh, and the first pointer I had to something else in Africa, something far closer to my own inner realities than I had ever cared to contemplate, I found in a folk story of the Ashanti, still to my mind the most disturbing of all the Africans.

It told the tale of a poor hunter who, miraculously elevated one day to kingship, found himself transported to a luxurious palace and given the freedom of the hedonist life. His every wish was granted, his every need supplied, except only that for reasons unexplained he was forbidden ever to open a particular door in the palace. For years he did not care about this prohibition, happily living with his pleasures, but presently the door began to nag at him, and the ban assumed an importance in his thoughts altogether out of proportion to his freedoms. At last he could stand it no longer, and brushing aside his attendants, ignoring the warnings of sages and the restraining rattles of witch doctors' monkey bones, he opened the door and looked inside. What did he see? Only himself, all in rags in a corner of the room, the identical poor hunter of long before.

This story powerfully affected me, and I began to see behind the crudities and irritations of African life far deeper realities. I shifted my viewpoint. I still would not want to be ruled by Africans, but then they did not want to rule me. I saw now, behind the tiresome hilarities and the boasting, emotions far more febrile and vulnerable—fears and embarrassments I had not grasped before, insights I could not share, traditions I could never master. As my Pole had illustrated infinity by his parallel of the universe, so it dawned upon me that within the African mind there might be exact equivalents of my own conceptions. I saw myself as an Anglo-Welsh amateur, curiously compounded, blissfully happy on one level, deeply unhappy on another, contorted with mixed fancies and torments, fired by patriotism, inhibited by upbringing, inexhaustibly in love; and I began to see that there could be African versions of myself, mirror-images of me, whose preoccupations were just as obsessive, and whose emotions, beneath the fluff and the racket, were at least as profound.

So over the years, on repeated visits, I came to regard black Africa as a solace, and after a time, I found, the Africans no longer bored me with their gregarious bonhomie, but revealed to me more frankly a deeper stillness of their spirit. This growing empathy has been very good for me. I do not subscribe to the fashionable ecology, disbelieving in the necessity of wildernesses, and accepting man and all his works as the dominant force of nature. But I have come to see within the mystery of the African genius, veiled as it is by superstition, fear, and resentment, something of the magic of the earth itself. I see how those subtleties have been preserved by the calm of the African landscapes, the incomparable parade of the African stars, the beat of the water-fowl wings over the African lakes, and that scented heavy silence, broken only by the chafing of the crickets and the squawks of unlikely night-birds, which falls upon Africa when the sun goes down.

Later I came to apply these specifics to myself, but it was years before I recognized their curative properties. In a Kenya game park once I saw a family of wart-hogs waddling ungainly and in a tremendous hurry across the grass. Contemptuous though I am of those who find animals comic, or degrade them in zoos and circuses, or in the name of science, still I could not help laughing at this quaint spectacle. My African companion rightly rebuked me. "You should not laugh at them," he said. "They are beautiful to each other."

I spent half my life traveling in foreign places. I did it because I liked it, and to earn a living, and I have only lately come to see that incessant wandering as an outer expression of my inner journey. I have never doubted, though, that much of the emotional force, what the Welsh call *hwyl*, that men spend in sex, I sublimated in travel—perhaps even in movement itself, for I have always loved speed, wind, and great spaces. (Discussing in print once Sydney Smith's conception of heaven as eating *pâté de foie gras* to the sound of trumpets, I have described my own as bowling across Castile in my Rolls-Royce of the day, with the roof open, Mendelssohn's Violin Concerto on the radio, and my Abyssinian cat beside me on the front seat. A reader of different impulses wrote to say that he agreed with the car, the place, and even the music, but as a companion would want something a damned sight more interesting than a *cat*.)

But it could not work forever. The instinct to keep moving played itself out, as I grew older, and as a cat expecting kittens prepares herself a nest in barn or chimney, so there came a time for me when the wandering had to stop. My time was approaching. My manhood was meaningless. With Elizabeth's loving help I abandoned the attempt to live on as a male, and took the first steps towards a physical change of sex.

TWELVE

CHANGING SEX · HORMONAL EFFECTS A PRECARIOUS CONDITION · SELF-PROTECTION · RULES

Our children were safely growing; I felt I had, so far as I could, honored the responsibilities of my marriage; rather than go mad, or kill myself, or worst of all perhaps infect everyone around me with my profoundest melancholy, I would accept Dr. Benjamin's last resort, and have my body altered.

Nobody in the history of humankind has changed from a true man to a true woman, if we class a man or a woman purely by physical concepts. Hermaphrodites may have shifted the balance of their ambiguity, but nobody has been born with one complete body and died with the other. When I say, then, that I now began a change of sex, I speak in shorthand. What was about to happen was that my body would be made as female as science could contemplate or nature permit, to reset (as I saw it) the pointer of my sex more sensibly and accurately along the scale of my gender. Doctors, whose conception of these matters is often simplistic to the degree of obscurantism, have devised many tests for the determination of sex, and divided the concept into several categories. There is anatomical sex, the most obvious: breasts, vagina, womb, and ovaries for the female, penis and testicles for the male. There is chromosomal sex, the most fundamental: the nuclear composition of the body, which need not necessarily conform to the anatomy, but which is accepted as a convenient rule of thumb for such purposes as international sport. There is hormonal sex, the chemical balance of male and female. There is psychological sex, the way people respond to the world, and feel themselves to be.

I was not much interested in these criteria, for I regarded sex merely as the tool of gender, and I believed that for me as for most people the interplay between the two lay very close to personality, not to be measured by blood tests or Freudian formulae. All I wanted was liberation, or reconciliation—to live as myself, to clothe myself in a more proper body, and achieve Identity at last. I would not hurry. First I would discover if it were feasible. Slowly, carefully, with infinite precaution against betrayal, I began the chemical experiments by which I would lose many of my male characteristics, and acquire some of the female; then, if all went well, several years later I would take the last step, and have the change completed by surgery.

To myself I had been woman all along, and I was not going to change the truth of me, only discard the falsity. But I *was* about to change my form and apparency—my status too, perhaps my place among my peers, my attitudes no doubt, the reactions I would evoke, my reputation, my manner of life, my prospects, my emotions, possibly my abilities. I was about to adapt my body from a male conformation to a female, and I would shift my public role altogether, from the role of a man to the role of a woman. It is one of the most drastic of all human changes, unknown until our own times, and even now experienced by very few; but it seemed only natural to me, and I embarked upon it only with a sense of thankfulness, like a lost traveler finding the right road at last.

These events had been arcanely forecast to me. A Xosa wise woman, telling my future in her dark hut of the Transkei, had assured me long before that I would one day be woman too; and a reader of mine in Stockholm had repeatedly warned me that the King of Sweden was changing my sex by invisible rays. As you know, I had myself long seen in my quest some veiled spiritual purpose, as though I was pursuing a Grail or grasping Oneness. There was, however, nothing mystic about the substances I now employed to achieve my ends. Since the discovery of hormones early in the century, they had been successfully isolated and reproduced; and the pills I now took three times a day, as I started on my journey, were made in Canada from the urine of pregnant mares.

Dr. Benjamin prescribed them for me, and I took them with unfailing regularity for the next eight years, supplemented by artificial female hormones too. Hasty calculation suggests to me that between 1964 and 1972 I swallowed at least 12,000 pills, and absorbed into my system anything up to 50,000 milligrams of female matter. Much of this doubtless went to waste, the body automatically discharging what it cannot absorb; the rest took its effect, and turned me gradually from a person who looked like a healthy male of orthodox sexual tendencies, approaching middle age, into something perilously close to a hermaphrodite, apparently neither of one sex nor the other, and more or less ageless. I was assured that this was a reversible process, and that if after some years of trial I decided to go no further, I might gradually revert to the male again; but of course the more frankly feminine I became the happier I was, object of curiosity though I became to the world at large, and embarrassment I fear, though they never dreamt of showing it, to Elizabeth and the children.

The change was infinitely gradual. I felt like a slow-motion Jekyll and Hyde, tinkering with test-tubes and retorts in my dark laboratory; but the effects were so subtle that they seemed not to be induced at all, were not noticed for years by everyday acquaintances, and seemed to be part of the natural process of aging. Except that, fortunately, they worked backwards, and rejuvenated me. The first result was not exactly a feminization of my body, but a stripping away of the rough hide in which the male person is clad. I do not mean merely the body hair, nor even the leatheriness of the skin, nor all the hard protrusion of muscle; all these indeed vanished over the next few years, but there went with them something less tangible too, which I know now to be specifically masculine—a kind of unseen layer of accumulated resilience, which provides a shield for the male of the species, but at the same time deadens the sensations of the body. It is as though some protective substance has been sprayed onto a man from a divine aerosol, so that he is less immediately in contact with the air and the sun, more powerfully compacted within his own resources.

This suggestion, for it is really hardly more, was now stripped from me, and I felt at the same time physically freer and more vulnerable. I had no armor. I seemed to feel not only the heat and the cold more, but also the stimulants of the world about me. I relished the goodness of the sun in a more directly physical way, and for the first time in my life saw the point of lazing about on beaches. The keenness of the wind cut me more spitefully. It was as though I could feel the very weight of the air pressing on my person, or eddying past, and I thought that if I closed my eyes now the presence of the moonlight would cool my cheek. I was far lighter in weight, but I was lighter in motion too, not so brilliantly precipitate as I had been on Everest, but airier, springier. It was rather as though my sense of gravity had shifted, making me more delicate or subtle of balance. I dreamt frequently of levitation, and found it curiously more easy to slip around a corner when I observed some dour acquaintance approaching me up the street, as though for a moment or two I could levitate in real life.

All this helped to make me younger. It was not merely a matter of *seeming* younger; except in the matter of plain chronology, it was actually true. I was enjoying that dream of the ages, a second youth. My skin was clearer, my cheeks were rosier, my tread was lighter, my figure was slimmer. More important, I was actually starting again. It was as though I had slipped the gears of life, returning to an earlier cycle for a second time round; or had reached one of those repeats in a sonata which start identically, but end in piquant difference. Life and the world looked new to me. Even my relationship with Elizabeth, which soon lost its last elements of physical contact, assumed a new lucidity. My body seemed to be growing more complex, more quivering in its responses, but my spirit felt simpler. I had loved animals all my life, but I felt closer to them now, and sometimes I even found myself talking to the garden flowers, wishing them a Happy Easter, or thanking them for the fine show they made ("Was the whole process," asked one of my publisher's readers, commenting upon this passage in a first draft of the book, "affecting her mind a little?"—but no, I had been talking to my typewriter for years, not always in such grateful terms.)

At first people thought I looked inexplicably young, consulted *Who's Who* to compound their bewilderment, or unkindly likened me to Dorian Gray (whose picture grew old while he stayed young, you will remember, until the dreadful reversal of the final chapter). I had presented in the past a figure not undistinguished in its slight way, and was accustomed to the respect which an educated Briton could expect, at least in those days, all over the world. People were not often cheeky to me, still less condescending. Taxi-drivers called me "Guv" sometimes, secretaries took their glasses off, and guests in my house, knowing my savage aversion to tobacco, sometimes hid behind trees for surreptitious cigarettes. Now things began to change. I noticed in the reaction of people something avuncular or even patronizing. Taxi-drivers were surprised when I asked to be taken to my club, and said it didn't seem the place for me. Waitresses were motherly, and expected only modest tips. When Elizabeth and I dined together as often as not they gave the bill to her, and once when I was visiting one of my sons at Eton, and we were coveting a stuffed owl through the window of an antique shop (it stands beside me now), a passing school matron asked if it wasn't time the pair of us were back indoors.

But after a year or two the character of my metamorphosis became more apparent, and I began to look not simply younger, but more feminine. Now not just the texture but the shape of my body began to change. My waist narrowed, my hips broadened rather, and my small breasts blossomed like blushes. My hair, which had been crisp and curly, now grew softer and longer, and my posture and demeanor, though I did nothing consciously to adapt them, became each month more womanly. I became a somewhat equivocal figure. Some people assumed me to be a homosexual, some thought me a kind of hybrid, some supposed me to be a woman already, and opened doors for me. I had reached a halfway mark, and probably looked on the outside more or less how I had always felt within.

Stripped of my clothes, I was a chimera, half male, half female, an object of wonder even to myself. I could no longer swim in our river at home, one of the great pleasures of my life, and I had to abandon my lifelong habit of plunging into whatever pool, lake, or ocean I came across in my travels. Sometimes, though, on fine summer days, I made a pilgrimage to a little lake I knew high in the mountains called the Glyders, in North Wales. There I could bathe alone. Early in the morning I would scramble up the hills, to where the lake stood sedgy and serene beside a gentle col. The light would be pale and misty, the air tangy, and all around the Welsh hills lay blue in the morning. The silence was absolute. There I would take my clothes off, and all alone in that high world stand for a moment like a figure of mythology, monstrous or divine, like nobody else those mountains have ever seen; and when, gently wading through the reeds, and feeling the icy water rise past my loins to my trembling breasts, I fell into the pool's embrace, sometimes I thought the fable might well end there, as it would in the best Welsh fairy tales.

I found the androgynous condition in some ways a nightmare, but in others an adventure. Imagine if you can the moment when, having passed through the customs at Kennedy Airport, New York, I approach the security check. Dressed as I am in jeans and a sweater, I have no idea to which sex the policemen will suppose me to belong, and must prepare my responses for either decision. I feel their silent appraisal down the corridor as I approach them, and as they search my sling bag I listen hard for a "Sir" or a "Ma'am" to decide my course of conduct. Beyond the corridor, I know, the line divides, men to the male frisker, women to the female, and so far I have no notion which to take. On either side a careful examination would reveal ambiguities of anatomy, and I would be plunged into all the ignominies of inquiry and examination, the embarrassments all round, the amusement or contempt, the gruff apologies and the snigger behind my back. But "Sir" or "Madam" comes there none, and through the curtain I diffidently go, to stand there at the bifurcation of the passengers undetermined. An awful moment passes. Everyone seems to be looking at me. Then "Move along there, lady, please, don't hold up the traffic"—and instantly I join the female queue, am gently and (as it proves) not all that skillfully frisked by a girl who thanks me for my co-operation, and emerge from another small crisis pleased (for of course I have hoped for this conclusion all along) but shaken too.

It is a precarious condition. One must live not for the day, but for the moment, swiftly adjusting to circumstance. During a journey in South Africa once I was told at lunchtime that I must wear a collar and tie in the dining room, at dinner that I must not enter wearing trousers. On a train from Euston to Bangor a man who had just been asking me if I had played cricket at Oxford was taken aback when the waiter, placing my soup before me, said, "There you are then, love, enjoy it!" In Denver a lady who began selling me a suitcase as a man developed doubts in the course of the transaction, and subtly shifting her sales technique, from the dogmatic to the confiding, ended by asking me if she couldn't interest me in a new handbag too. Very unexpected people, like New York harbormen, or linotype operators, put their arms around my waist and declared their affection, but just as often I never did discover what sex people supposed me to be, and we parted on a plane of mutual mystification. My colleague H. V. Morton, when I called upon him for the first time at his house in the Cape, was told by his maid that a lady had come to see him, and likened me when I left to Ariel, insubstantial, ill-defined, and always on the move.

Reactions to my ambivalence varied greatly from nation to nation, or culture to culture. Among the guileless peoples the problem was minimal. They simply asked. After a flight from Darjeeling to Calcutta, for instance, during which I had enjoyed the company of an Indian family, the daughter walked over to me at the baggage counter when we had disembarked. "I hope you won't mind my asking," she simply and politely said, "but my brothers wish to know whether you are a boy or a girl." In Mexico, after staring hard for several days, and eying my sparse traveler's wardrobe with bewilderment, a deputation of housemaids came to my door one day. "Please tell us," they said, "whether you are a lady or a gentleman." I whipped up my shirt to show my bosom, and they gave me a bunch of flowers when I left. "Are you a man or a woman?" asked the Fijian taxi-driver as he drove me from the airport. "I am a respectable, rich, middle-aged English widow," I replied. "Good," he said, "just what I want," and put his hand upon my knee.

Americans generally assumed me to be a female, and cheered me up with small attentions. Englishmen, I think, especially Englishmen of the educated classes, found the ambiguity in itself beguiling: as I became less apparently homosexual, and more evidently something more esoteric, I found their responses ever more agreeable, enlivened always by that instant flicker of amused attraction which every woman knows and no man can quite imagine. Frenchmen were curious, and tended to engage me in inquisitive conversation, neatly skirting the issues with small talk until the moment came for a swift oblique dart to the heart of things: "You are married, yes? Where is your—er—your wife—your husband, is it?" Italians, frankly unable to conceive the meaning of such a phenomenon, simply stared boorishly, or nudged each other in piazzas. Greeks were vastly entertained. Arabs asked me to go for walks with them. Scots looked shocked. Germans looked worried. Japanese did not notice.

But two classes of person put the puzzle into quite different perspectives. In all the Western countries young people did not seem to care which I was, expecting me it seemed to decide for myself, expressing no surprise, and treating me with equal familiarity whichever way I opted. And the black people of Africa, men and women alike, made me feel that there was to my condition an element of privilege. They viewed me with shining eyes. Close as they were to still stranger things, to music I could not hear, visions I could not see, they treated me as a lesser mystery, and cherished me. Old men held my hands for long thoughtful moments, as though they were deriving merit from the touch. Women bade me sit by them, not for any special reason, simply to share my presence. I was once walking down the steps to the wharf at Freetown, in Sierra Leone, where long ago the liberated slaves were disembarked to begin their new lives in the colony. I was pursued by a chattering and curious crowd of children, dogging my every step, laughing and kicking stones about the place. I liked their merry company, but at the quayside a tall watchman of the waterfront, constituting himself my guardian, shooed them all away. "Go," he said, "go. This Person is Alone"—as though I was, in my strange isolation, not altogether corporeal.

I came to accept this unreality. In the only novel I have read about gender confusion, Geoff Brown's tragic *I Know What I Want*, the hero/heroine at one point determines himself to be no more than a freak, "queer, miserable, hunched-up." I was resolute never to think of myself in this way. The world could take me or leave me, and one day, I was sure now, I would emerge from this bizarre chrysalis if not a butterfly, at least a presentable moth. If life gives you a lemon, as an American sage once remarked, make yourself a lemonade. In the meantime, of course, I was sometimes wounded. I was not an exhibitionist by nature, and though scarcely a shrinking violet either, preferred to attract attention for more straightforward reasons. I was more easily wounded than I cared to admit even to myself, and my family often sensed it, and suffered with me. "That man's staring at me," my little Tom once said, squeezing my hand as if for reassurance; but I knew he was staring at *me*, and so I think did Tom.

It was in Kashmir that I first allowed my unreality to act as its own cloak around me, or more appositely perhaps as the veil of a Muslim woman, which protects her from so many nuisances, and allows her to be at her best or her worst inside. In that happy valley I found my status to be especially uncertain, and I seemed to grope my way through a web of misunderstandings, *doubles entendres*, and miscellaneous embarrassments. The water-peddlers who sidled past my houseboat in their punts, suddenly appearing over the rail or through the dining-room windows like amphibians of the lake, found me at least as startling as I did them, and my entrepreneur host did not know from first to last whether his guest was male or female, answering inquiries about me only with a discreet and baffled shrug. To protect myself against these perplexities I went transcendental, and for the rest of my stay in limbo I used the device often in self-protection.

Of course I caught it from Kashmir itself, where for generations wise men have turned to fantasy as a protection against unhappiness. In Kashmir I learnt to discount time, and dismiss truth for the moment. I answered questions as I liked. I let fall all those mental inhibitions which, though invaluable in most situations, were proving temporarily inadequate in mine. I abandoned the sense of shame which had driven me to so many exertions. I entered, I suppose, some other plane, and spent long restful hours in it, examining small water-weeds upon the deck of the houseboat, or deep in that other textbook of the Eightfold Path, *Pride and Prejudice*.

For you must not suppose that I had gone off my head. Far from it. I had entered this new state quite consciously, and having discovered it in Kashmir, developed it later as a technique. I was for the time being a kind of nonhuman, a sprite or monster, as you wish; so when the world oppressed me I left it, and wandering through other fields of sensibility, like the Moguls before me I insulated myself against misfortune. Harmless lying, I found, was itself a panacea. Either people believed me when I said I had a unicorn at home, or they thought me crazy, or they called me a liar, or they accepted the fancy for itself; and by offering them four distinct choices, the lie diverted their attention from mistier enigmas behind, and excused me too from specifics. After all, my life was one long protest against the separation of fact from fantasy: fantasy *was* fact, I reasoned, just as mind was body, or imagination truth.

I was not alone, anyway, in finding solace in this way. Half the world at that time was trying to soothe itself with drugs and hallucinations, and withdrawing ever more eccentrically from reality. In Kanpur, in India, I came across a man with whom I felt an instant affinity, so similar was his system of emancipation to my own. That he was deeply unhappy was obvious, but he numbed his misery by touching things. Day and night he wandered the streets of the city, earnestly and methodically touching windows, doorposts, lamp standards, apparently to a set of unwritten rules. Sometimes he appeared to feel that he had neglected the task, and did a street all over again, paying a still more diligent attention to the doorknobs, and I was told that there was scarcely an alley of the inner city where his busy activity was not familiar. I spoke to him one morning, but he responded only with an engaging preoccupied smile, as if to say that, though some other time it would be delightful to have a chat, that day he simply hadn't a moment to spare.

I was sure now that in the end surgery would rescue me from these varied predicaments, and Elizabeth too viewed my fluctuating moods philosophically, knowing that they would reconcile themselves one day. I had learnt, though, that the few reputable surgeons who would perform the operation in England or America decreed strict preliminary conditions. The patient must not be psychotic. He must understand the procedures. He must be physically compatible to the new role. He must not be cruelly abandoning or betraying dependents. He must already have acquired, by protracted hormone treatment, the secondary female characteristics, and lost the male ones. Above all he must have lived for some years in the role of his new sex, and proved that socially and economically it was possible.

I did not greatly care whether my surgeon was reputable, but still these rules seemed sensible to me. I had heard of people who, in the despair of their predicament, had rushed all unprepared into what they called a change of sex, and by that violent wrenching of nature had made themselves only the unhappier. Most of the criteria, I felt, I satisfied already. Those thousands of pills had transformed my physique: if I was not a woman, I was certainly a strange sort of man. For all my ventures into another reality I was still not insane. My children were growing up in the knowledge of my ambiguity, and nothing on earth would persuade me to betray them. Economically it made no difference whether I was male or female.

The time had come, I thought, to move a stage further. I had reached the frontier between the sexes, and it was time for me tentatively to explore life on the far side.

living in this way, and many friends came to call upon me, or to gather material for common-room anecdotes.

Was it not an astonishing, exciting, alarming, erotic, disturbing experience, I am asked, to dress as a woman at last? Not particularly. It was very pleasant for me, partly because I liked the stuffs, the colors, and the flow of women's clothes, but chiefly because it seemed to me symbolic of my progress. The transvestite gets an unfailing sexual *frisson* from wearing the clothes of the opposite sex, just as the profoundest source of his pleasure is the knowledge of his hidden phallus, potent and lurking beneath his disguise. But the true transsexual feels no more than a sense of relief, when he appears as a woman at last. Dr. Stoller reports the case of a child in America who was assumed at birth to be a girl, but who felt herself undeviatingly to be a boy until, in adolescence, she was found to possesss undeveloped male organs. Her life had been a perpetual struggle to express her conviction of boyhood, but when at last the truth of her claims was recognized, and she was told that she was in fact a male, the psychologists were intrigued to discover that she displayed no particular sense of triumph. "Rather, her attitude was as if to say, 'Yes. Very good. Thank you. I am not surprised.' "

So it was with me. I was merely a stage nearer the unraveling of my conundrum. I was mending a discrepancy, smoothing an incongruity, and I found that when people took me to be unquestionably a woman, a sense of rightness calmed and satisfied me. I looked a mannish sort of female, I expect, for my face was still lean and narrow in the male way, but I felt far less obtrusive in skirts than I did in trousers. I soon discovered, too, that people see in you what they expect to see: they knew me down there only as a woman, and if I had come down the street wearing flying boots and a crash helmet, woman they would have thought me still. I felt myself to be passing through an anteroom of fulfillment. I loathed the times when, leaving my little Oxford haven, I was obliged to return to ambiguity, and I found it harder and harder, crueller and crueller, to present myself as a male.

Still, my worst miseries were over now, and my preoccupations were, so to speak, largely logistical. I had to remember in which role I was known in any given circumstance. As I divided my life more absolutely between the sexes, there were many places in which I could not appear as a man, and vice versa. There were families who knew me only as a male, or only as a female, or as both—or some people at a dinner table might know the truth about me, but not others—or I might be a member of one society in this sex, of another in that. It was confusing. In London, where many people now knew me in both roles, I took to warning them in advance which way to expect me; sometimes, conversely, people would kindly inquire how I would prefer to be invited. The satirical magazine *Private Eye* said once that if I was bidden to a function "dressed informally" it meant that I was expected *en femme*, but unfortunately no such handy code was practicable, and often I had to play my gender fugue altogether by ear, hoping that its various themes would be harmoniously resolved on the night.

Sometimes the arena of my ambivalence was uncomfortably small. At the Travellers' Club, for example, I was obviously known as a man of sorts—women were only allowed on the premises at all during a few hours of the day, and even then were hidden away as far as possible in lesser rooms or alcoves. But I had another club, only a few hundred yards away, where I was known only as a woman, and often I went directly from one to the other, imperceptibly changing roles on the way—"Cheerio, sir," the porter would say at one club, and "Hello, madam," the porter would greet me at the other. Some institutions I joined in both capacities, and as I eased myself gradually out of the male role, so I resigned the one membership and retained the other. Inevitably I was caught out once or twice: I shall never forget the mingled consternation, bewilderment, and disbelief with which one very orthodox fellow-traveller, catching sight of me outside Fortnum's swinging along Piccadilly in my bright blue coat, stood stock-still in his tracks to watch me pass—which I did, I may say, with the blithest of smiles, for I was past caring by then.

One day, clearly, it must all be public knowledge, and to ease the process Elizabeth and I deliberately widened the range of our confidants. In Oxford I told my old tutor at Christ Church, only to discover that he had learnt the tale already *via* Harvard. He told the Dean for me, and thereafter when I went to evensong, and met good old Dr. Simpson in the porch, he would bow to me most gallantly. In London one by one I told less intimate friends about myself, and so experienced a sequence of meetings which, while they became progressively more ordinary for me, were clearly unnerving experiences for them. They did not know what to expect. What would I look like, as a woman? Would I be bawdy or bold, pitiful or painful? I have often imagined the conversation with which, huddled slightly alarmed in their taxi, husband and wife crawled through London towards me, half wishing perhaps that they had never started, but still undeniably curious as to what they would find. And I can see now the nervous pallor of their faces as, entering the lobby of my club, they looked around helplessly to see which of the waiting members might conceivably be me—and the relief too, I like to think, when they discovered me to be surprisingly like the person they had always known, if not unembarrassing, at least unembarrassed!

Not all my friends, of course, were so circumspect, and some treated the whole affair as a phenomenon of purely objective interest. "Welcome to the underground," said I to one colleague, as we stood alone a moment after our revelatory meeting. "It doesn't seem very underground to me," he replied, and from that day he encouraged me to think of my metamorphosis not merely as a remedial measure, but as a truth in its own right—a precedent of sorts, which I might use as I would. Elizabeth too helped me to think of the experience as something to be valued in itself; and it is true that though that double world of mine offered hazards and humiliations of its own, still it was full of fascination. It suggested to me not the solution, but more the dissolving of my conundrum. The riddle seemed to be falling into its separate parts, ready to be reassembled in a better light. No wonder strangers often smiled at me in the street; for I was full of an expectant happiness, half secret, half shared—not unlike pregnancy, I suppose, or the last marvelous week in the writing of a book.

Now I told the State of my condition—the Department of Health and Social Security, the Passport Office. Unbending from the dour austerity of its addresses in Whitaker's Almanac, it responded with an unexpected flexibility. When the time came, the Establishment assured me, my new sexual role would be officially recognized. In the meantime, I might be issued with new documents to see me through the transitional phase. I took a new Christian name by statutory declaration, adopting after long discussion and experiment the still androgynous Jan, not because I wished always to straddle the sexes, but because I thought it would make the change of habit less abrupt for my relatives and friends (and perhaps I thought, too, at the back of my mind, that if I failed to succeed in my new persona I could somehow retreat into the old). My bank, to whose manager I had long before confided my secret, laconically changed me from a Mr. to a Miss. The Oxford County Council gave me a new driving license. The Welfare Officer of the Passport Office sent me a passport without any indication of sex at all—compounding as it happened, during my last year of intersexual travel, the mystification of foreign officials.

Though I had been armed with medical certificates for many years, and was fortified by assurances from the Medical Law Society, still these fresh credentials gave me new confidence. The fear of ignominy was never, I suppose, quite absent from my mind. Now I felt that society, if it could not yet quite accept me, still recognized me for what I was. I took to living almost entirely as a woman, only returning into epicene ambiguity at home in Wales. This meant that Elizabeth and I had to devise a new overt relationship. We could not easily be sisters, for she was Mrs. Morris, I was Miss. We did not wish to be merely friends, for that would deny me any kinship with my children. So we settled for sisters-in-law, the nearest to the truth that we could devise. I had in very truth become my own sister, and as the personality, even in time the memory of James began to fade from my life, so I became a kind of adoring if interfering aunt to my children, and a relative linked neither by blood nor carnality to Elizabeth.

How to tell the children what was happening was the

hardest of all our problems. That *something* was happening was very apparent, for though I never appeared before them in women's clothes, more often than not I was treated as a woman in their company. We were not too afraid of their own reactions; they were past the most vulnerable years of their childhood, the elder ones indeed almost men themselves, and we placed our faith as always in the healing power of love. More distressing, we thought, was the danger that they might be teased or mocked at school. My eldest son Mark tells me that he first guessed the truth by discovering in our library a shelf of books on transsexuality—carefully placed there, as it happened, so that he *would* guess. The others discovered it all, I think, gradually—by hint or by allusion, by talk among themselves, and finally by my own self-revelation. Helped along the way by sensitive teachers, they seemed to escape the miseries of school taunting, and the more feminine I became, the closer to my own reality, the closer I felt to them too. There was no moment of instant trauma in our relationship, no moment when, standing before them as a man one day, I reappeared suddenly as a woman. The process was infinitely slow and subtle, and through it all anyway, as I hope they sensed, I remained the same affectionate self.

In the summer of 1971 an American publisher invited me to write a short book about the Cascade Mountains, as one of an ecologically improving series they were preparing about the world's wildernesses. The Cascades are a volcanic range running from British Columbia to northern California, and I accepted the commission with misgivings, for I distrusted the conservationist cult in America, and was by no means a lover of *all* Nature's works. Also the Cascades, though some of their landscapes are among the most magnificent on earth, are thickly covered with conifers—"Mighty Monarchs of the Northwest," as the brochures call them—and infested everywhere with mosquitoes. Still, the travel urge was upon me, I always welcome a trip to the States, and buying ourselves rucksacks, boots, food as supplied to space travelers, and anti-insect squirters, Elizabeth and I set off together to look at the place.

It was our first long journey aboard as two women, my last legally as a man, and it was the happiest of my life. How merrily we traveled! What fun the Oregonians gave us! How cheerfully we swopped badinage with boatmen and lumberjacks, flirtatious garage hands and hospitable trappers! We wandered free as air through the forests, cursing the bugs and refusing to admit the worst in our vacuum-packed beans. We took the steamer to the head of Lake Chelan, that loveliest of America's lakes, curving like a fiord into the heart of the Glacier Peak country, and we sped lavishly up the Seattle freeway in our rented limousine, eating apples all the way. I never felt so liberated, or more myself, nor was I ever more fond of Elizabeth. "Come on in, girls," the motel men would say, and childish though I expect it sounds to you, silly in itself, perhaps a little pathetic, possibly grotesque, still if they had touched me with an accolade of nobility, or clad me ceremonially in crimson, I could not have been more flattered.

The book was still-born, all the same, for in Chapter Three the publishers discovered my unquenchable antipathy to the Douglas Fir.

FOURTEEN

CONCERNING SURGERY

There remained the surgery—which, while it might make no difference to my status in the mind of God, would certainly affect it in the eye of man. I had male organs still, and for all those thousands of milligrams of female substance deposited in me down the years, still my body was producing male hormones in rearguard desperation. Before I could live in equanimity always and only as a woman, I must find myself a surgeon.

The operation called "sex change" had lately become relatively respectable. Until a few years before it had been disreputable indeed, considered by most surgeons to be a cross between a racket, an obscenity, and a very expensive placebo. It was, wrote one London practitioner in the 1950s, as though when a man said he was Nelson, you were to cut off his arm to satisfy his illusion. For thirty years after the Lili Elbe case there were few attempts to change a person's sex, and surgeons in most countries would not contemplate such an operation. In 1951 the American George Jorgensen managed to achieve surgery in Denmark, and fellow-sufferers everywhere tried to emulate him, but the doctors reacted more forbiddingly still. They were frightened by the threat of publicity. They were repelled by the weird gallimaufry that pestered them, along with the true transsexuals —exhibitionists in search of new themes, homosexuals wishing to legalize themselves, female impersonators and miscellaneous paranoiacs. They were unsure of the legal implications: in most countries the law was hazy about the definition of sex, and even obscurer about the legality of trying to change it. They were afraid that their patients might regret the change and become more psychotic than ever, besides very likely suing their surgeons for mayhem. The psychological jolt of the operation would be so terrific, the later demands upon the patient so severe, that even the most sympathetic surgeons would not operate without years of pretreatment and observation.

By 1972, when my time came, the climate of medical opinion had shifted. Thanks largely to the persuasion of Dr. Benjamin in New York City, many more doctors now conceded that surgery might after all be the right approach to a problem which seemed to be becoming more common, and was plainly insoluble in absolute terms. The old psychiatric treatments had been discredited. The degrading practices of aversion treatment were admitted to have no effect upon true transsexuals. The usual formulae of sex determination, acceptable though they might be to judges or Olympic referees, were increasingly recognized as inadequate, as the complexities of gender and identity became each year more apparent but more baffling.

In America several university hospitals had started gender-identity units, where surgery was used as a last resort, and in England too several hospitals now operated upon transsexuals. At least 600 people, of both original sexes, had undergone surgery in the United States; at least one had been ordered to do so by a court of law. Perhaps another 150 had been operated upon in Britain, many of them free under the National Health system. The technical procedures were well established. In the case of those who were born males, the penis and testicles were removed and a vagina was created, either simultaneously or in later surgery; functionally the patient was left more or less in the condition of a woman who has undergone a total hysterectomy. Orgasm was possible, because the erotic zones retained their sensitivity, but not of course conception, for nobody had yet succeeded in transplanting ovaries, let alone a womb.

This is what I now planned to have done to myself. I had long been assured by my London doctors that when the time came, there would be no difficulty. But when, in the spring of 1972, I felt myself ready for the last hurdle, and my family too, I discovered an unexpected snag. The surgeon who interviewed me, and who accepted me for surgery at the Charing Cross Hospital, declined to operate until Elizabeth and I were divorced. I saw his point, for he could not know the nature of the relationship between us, and indeed I recognized that we must be divorced in the end. But after a lifetime of fighting my own battles I did not feel in a mood to offer my destiny like a sacrifice upon the benches of Her Majesty's judges. Who knew what degradations we might both endure? What business was it of theirs, anyway?

No, I resolved, I would make the rules now. We would end our marriage in our own time, lovingly, and I would go for my surgery, as I had gone for so many consolations and distractions before, to foreign parts beyond the law.

FIFTEEN

TREFAN · THE LAST SUMMER · ON WELSHNESS · TO THE MAGICIAN

But first, for my last good-byes to maleness, I turned to the little country to which I felt I most truly belonged, and went home to my loves in Wales. There up a long and bumpy lane, protected by ash trees, beeches, and tumble-down oaks, stood the house I had bought for us long before, Trefan at Llanystumdwy in Caernarvonshire. Its land ran damp and brackeny to the river Dwyfor, which, rising in the hills only seven or eight miles above, tumbled swiftly through rock pool and gorge to empty into Cardigan Bay a mile or two below. Behind the house one could see the mountains, green and brown in summer, in winter often covered in snow, and above the first ridge the triangular summit of Snowdon protruded, so clear when the sky was right that one could sometimes make out the smoke-puffs of the funicular railway laboring up the north flank. In front of the house, across park and meadowland, lay the sea: through a gap in the trees the islands of St. Tidwal showed, and at night a lighthouse flashed reassuringly, white and red alternately, every twenty seconds.

Here I spent the last summer of my manhood. For me it will always be the most beautiful house in the world, and though I have since sold the Plas itself, keeping only some of the outbuildings, still Trefan will always be home to me. Architecturally it was hardly distinguished, but it had an easy, amateur air to it that I liked. Its east elevation was accomplished enough, looking like a comfortable Georgian rectory with its climbing magnolia and bay window, but the north side, where the front door stood, was palpably unprofessional—a gaunt, very Welsh façade, one floor too high for elegance, with a funny pillared porch in a manner more neo- than Classical, and rows of windows, oblong and many-paned, such as children like to draw. The house was white, and with its multitudinous diverse chimneys, its rambled outhouses, and its serried fenestration, seemed from a distance to lie lumpishly among its trees. But it was instinct with *baraka*, that scented concept of the Arab mind which means at once blessed and blessing, full of grace in itself and able to bestow grace upon others. It was a magic house.

Most people liked it best in the early spring, when the woods down to the river seemed to shift almost before one's eyes from snowdrop white to daffodil yellow to the shimmer of bluebells—when the rooks cawed furiously in the beeches, the garden woke to life in a splurge of rhododendrons, and the young lambs caught their heads five times a day in the fencing down the drive. I shall always remember it with the profoundest gratitude, though, as it was that May, that last May, in the last of my old summers.

Then after dinner Elizabeth and I would often wander down to the river, to watch the bats skimming and wheeling over the long pool, or hear the brown trout rising. The smell down there was an intoxication of river, weed, and moss, and at a point where the river flowed through a small steep gorge, we would clamber over a fallen tree trunk to a little island there, and find ourselves enclosed in the green, dark, rushing presence of the place. I so loved this spot that when I sold the house I kept the island, and there one day I shall be buried, beneath the epitaph HERE LIES JAN MORRIS OF TREFAN, AT THE END OF A HAPPY LIFE. For it was a restless, searching place, just right for me. Sometimes we made out the thrilling dark shapes of sea trout in the stream, as they ran up to the mountains from the sea; sometimes Sam the dog, snuffling around the wood, suddenly dashed into the darkness in pursuit of squirrels, or foxes, or lesser beasts of his own conception; sometimes glowworms lay like embers in the mold, and sometimes the faint pungent smell of a home-rolled cigarette, or the muffled click of a reel, told us that the poachers were out that night.

Then when the woods became too dark we would clamber up the bank beside the badger's sett, half expecting to hear a wheezing or grunting of protest from the warren beneath our feet, through the park field where the cows lay in the twilight munching, or the donkeys sidled after us in hope of affection, and round to the garden gate. Across the rough old lawn the house lay dimly white, with a night light glimmering in Susan's window, Mrs. Forward's television flickering from hers, and very likely the hastily extinguished flash of a torch from Tom's. If Mark was home we might hear Mahler or John Cage from his attic; if Henry was about we might meet him at the gate, back like a poacher himself with his rod and net from the long reach.

I always dragged out those last few yards to the house. It lay there like a dream for me, full of all I loved, my children and my animals, my books and my pictures, and blessed I thought like a healer's presence with a cure for my sickness.

I was home in Wales, but not for long. Where would I be next summer, I wondered? Whose lights would greet me then? We wound up the library clock, fed Sam and Menelik, scolded Tom as he deserved, cast a spell on Mark for using all the hot water, said good night to Henry as he fried himself a pancake, and went wistfully to our beds.

I call myself Anglo-Welsh, but I have always preferred the Welsh side of me to the English. When I looked Januslike to my double childhood view, it was always the line of the Black Mountains that compelled me, with their suggestion of mysteries and immensities beyond, and their reminder that there lay my strongest roots. If some of my troubles lay perhaps in dual affinities, so did much of my delight: for by and large the Anglo-Welsh, spared the heavier disciplines of pure Welshness, are exceedingly happy people, and concede it more readily than most. "What a marvelous life I've had!" said I in satisfaction to my neighbor Clough Williams-Ellis the architect, then in his eighties, when he came to my fortieth-birthday celebrations. "You've enjoyed it so far?" he beamed. "You wait for the *next* forty years!" He was a man who had known suffering in his time, but he was not ashamed to admit his compensating happinesses, and nor was I.

So that last summer at Trefan held no sadness for me, and the setting seemed almost allegorically suited to my denouement. As it happens I admire the English genius more than the Welsh. I prefer its humor, I admire its profounder poetry, its skeptical pragmatism, its confidence. But the Welsh in me had better qualified me for my tangled pilgrimage; for behind the Anglo-Welsh high spirits, I knew of deeper and darker instincts in myself, inherited from the heart of Wales

—itself a country which, caught in the lore of magicians and the web of bards, tenaciously struggling for eight hundred years to preserve its identity, is a bit of a conundrum too.

I knew myself for a romancer, in the Welsh way: not a romancer to achieve wicked ends, or even to achieve ends at all, but simply one whose instincts lead him now and then into fiction. "A Scotsman's truth," said the American Walter Hines Page, "is a straight line, but a Welshman's truth is more in the nature of a curve." Harmlessly bent in this way was my own conception of the truth, and it colored my reportage always as it gave piquancy to my self-awareness—for as a novelist manqué I probably romanced to myself more than to anyone. In Khartoum once a Sudanese Minister of National Guidance, soon to be shot for misdirecting the nation, offered me a succinct definition of my duties as a correspondent. They were, he said, to produce "thrilling, attractive, and good news, coinciding where possible with the truth." Erring as I did generally on the side of the ingratiating, I followed his posthumous guidelines fairly faithfully down the decades, and habitually accepted a fact as being more in the nature of a blur.

Then I often detected in myself that taste for the flamboyant which, in the Welsh especially, is so often a compensation for uncertainty. Coming as they do from distant and dramatic parts, the Welsh love to show off their distinction; translating the national *hwyl* into perpetual performance. Playing a part has always come naturally to me, if not one part, then another, and I have often indulged a weakness for display, in flowery adjectives or flashy cars. My guile, which had brought me safely through so many esoteric perils, is pure Welsh; so is the quick emotionalism, the hovering tear, the heart-on-sleeve, the touch of schmaltz, which has given my books the more sickly of their purple passages.

More deeply, I believe myself to have an extrasensory streak that springs directly from the strangeness of Wales. I see the dead sometimes; or more precisely, I see three dead persons, none of whom I knew well in life, and all of whom had always impressed me by their elusive, dappled quality—Gerard Fay the journalist, John Connell the biographer, Dennis Brain the horn player, all of whom I repeatedly encounter, walking through London, curiously embodied in the persons of men who, when I catch them up or meet them face to face, bear no resemblance to those ghosts at all.

I was never surprised by such phenomena. The Welsh are a disordered people, a people on the edge, and it came naturally to me to live outside the frame of things. Later that summer Henry went to India, planning to come back the following year to go to his University. When the time for his return approached, and we were expectantly awaiting news from him, I happened to see, standing beside the road outside Hereford, a figure astonishingly like him, loaded with rucksacks and pacing up and down the pavement with a proud thoughtful movement that was peculiarly his. I slowed down, and as I did so he looked up at me and smiled, gravely and without surprise; it was Henry's face, but subtly orientalized, Tibetanized perhaps, brown, its eyes a little slanted and its cheekbones high. I turned round, down the road, and went back for a second look; but this time the boy bore no resemblance to Henry at all, and took no notice of me.

A few weeks later we heard that Henry would not be coming home, but planned to stay in India instead; and there he remains to this day, the freest spirit of us all, teaching, writing, and learning in the Himalayan foothills. He was born when I was on Everest, and when I think about that messenger on the Hereford road, looking me so steady in the eye, I remember too the envoy I met long ago, alone and gently smiling, on the snows above Khumbu.

Against this beautiful, complex, haunting background, physical and spiritual, I prepared myself for the climax of my life. An irrepressible force had driven me through every barrier almost to the achievement of my inexplicable goal, and it was not spent yet. Love, luck, and resolution had saved me from suicide—for if there had been no hope of ending my life as a woman, I would certainly have ended it for myself as a man. Now those same happy attributes, which I seemed to draw from Trefan and from Wales like fuel from a pump, must see me over the last obstacle.

I booked myself a return ticket to Casablanca in Morocco, and waving a long farewell to the old house as I drove down the lane, in July, 1972, I flew away to Africa, where I had found solace before, and knew of a magician now.

SIXTEEN

CASABLANCA · IN THE CLINIC · A STUNNING THOUGHT · MADE NORMAL COMRADES! · NEW OUT OF AFRICA

Everybody in my predicament knew of Dr. B——. It was he who, over the years, had rescued hundreds, perhaps even thousands, of transsexuals from their wandering fate. Denied, all too often, surgery in their own countries, the more desperate sufferers roamed the world in search of salvation, to Mexico, to Holland, to Japan, knocking upon the doors of ever less distinguished surgeons, pleading, threatening, sometimes mutilating their own persons as a kind of blackmail. Many spent their life savings upon these tragic missions, and often they returned home irrevocably maimed, or no nearer their goal than they had been before. Nobody knows how many killed themselves. If once they got to Dr. B——, though, their desires if not their needs would be satisfied. He did not bother himself much with diagnosis or pretreatment, and expected handsome payment in advance; but his surgery was excellent, he asked no questions, and he imposed no conditions, legal or moralistic.

I did not know his address, but when I arrived in Casablanca I looked him up in the telephone book, and was told to come round to his clinic next afternoon. So I had time to wander round the town. As a city Casablanca is sometimes less than romantic, being mostly modern, noisy, and ugly in a pompous French colonial way. The experience I was to have there, though, struck me then as it strikes me now as romantic to a degree. It really was like a visit to a wizard. I saw myself, as I walked that evening through those garish streets, as a figure of fairy tale, about to be transformed. Duck into swan? Scullion into bride? More magical than any such transformation, I answered myself: man into woman. This was the last city I would ever see as a male. The office blocks might not look much like castle walls, nor the taxis like camels or carriages, but still I sometimes heard the limpid Arab music, and smelt the pungent Arab smells, that had for so long pervaded my life, and I could suppose it to be some city of fable, of phoenix and fantasy, in which transubstantiations were regularly effected, when the omens were right and the moon in its proper phase.

I called upon the British Consul in the morning. It occurred to me that I might die in the course of changing my sex, and I wanted him to let people know. He did not seem surprised. Always best, he said, to be on the safe side.

The clinic was not as I imagined it. I had rather hoped for something smoky in the bazaar, but it turned out to be in one of the grander modern parts of the city, one entrance on a wide boulevard, the other on a quiet residential back-street. Its more ordinary business was gynecology of one sort and another, and as I waited in the anteroom, reading *Elle* and *Paris-Match* with a less than absolute attention, I heard many natal sounds, from the muffled appeals of all-too-expectant mothers to the anxious pacings of paternity. Sometimes the place was plunged in utter silence, as Dr. B—— weighed somebody's destiny in his room next door; sometimes it broke into a clamor of women's Arabic, screechy and distraught somewhere down the corridor. At last the receptionist called for me, and I was shown into the dark and book-lined presence of the maestro.

He was exceedingly handsome. He was small, dark, rather intense of feature, and was dressed as if for some kind of beach activity. He wore a dark blue open-necked shirt, sports trousers, and games shoes, and he was very bronzed. He welcomed me with a bemused smile, as though his mind were in Saint-Tropez. What could he do for me, he asked? I told him I thought he probably knew very well. "Ah, I think that's so. You wish the operation. Very well, let us see you." He examined my organs. He plumped my breasts—"*Très, très bons.*" He asked if I was an athlete. "Very well," he said, "come in this evening, and we shall see what we can do. You know my fee? Ah well, perhaps you will discuss it with my receptionist—*Bien, au revoir*, until this evening!"

I paid the money, all in advance, and I signed the usual form absolving Dr. B—— from any responsibility if he happened to make a mess of it, and clutching my suitcase and a copy of that morning's *Times*, for I was not beaten yet, an hour later I was led along corridors and up staircases into the inner premises of the clinic. The atmosphere thickened as we proceeded. The rooms became more heavily curtained, more velvety, more voluptuous. Portrait busts appeared, I think, and there was a hint of heavy perfume. Presently I saw, advancing upon me through the dim alcoves of this retreat, which distinctly suggested to me the allure of a harem, a figure no less recognizably odalesque. It was Madame B——. She was dressed in a long white robe, tasseled I think around the waist, which subtly managed to combine the luxuriance of a caftan with the hygiene of a nurse's uniform, and she was blonde herself, and carefully mysterious.

She talked in a dreamy way, and was anxious to confirm that I had signed the travelers' checks. It was a lot of money, I ventured to murmur. "A lot of money! What would you have? He is a great surgeon, one of the great surgeons! What could you do," she theatrically demanded, throwing out her white arms like a celebrant, "if this great surgeon would not operate on you?" Go home to England, I said, and get it done there—"but let us not talk about the money," she interrupted hastily, and sweeping me into her ambiance she opened a small door set in a corner of what appeared to be her salon, and led the way down a spiral staircase. Instantly the atmosphere changed again. In the private quarters all had been shimmer and Chanel; down here, as we emerged into the corridor beneath, it was all clinical austerity. It was like going from the seraglio to the eunuch's quarters, not a bad simile I thought at the time.

It is true that the room numbers were painted on flowered enamel, the color scheme was pinkish, and in the corridor there stood a baby's crib, ribboned and cushioned. But an air of stern purpose informed the place, for these were the operating quarters. There was the operating theater itself, said Madame, gesturing towards a mercifully closed door, "and even now," she thrillingly added, "at this moment an American is under surgery. My husband works always." She opened the door of No. 5, the end room in the corridor, and bidding me a soft but frosty good night, for she was offended I think about the money, left me to my fate.

It was dark by now, and the room was uninviting. Its lighting was dim, its floor was less than scrupulously clean, and its basin, I soon discovered, never had hot water. Outside the window I could hear a faint rumble of traffic, and more precise street noises from the alley below. Inside, the clinic seemed to be plunged into a permanent silence, as though I was shut away and insulated from all other life—not far from the truth, either, for the bell did not work, and there was no other patient on the floor. Nobody came. I sat on the bed in the silence and did the *Times* crossword puzzle; for if these circumstances sound depressing to you, alarming even, I felt in my mind no flicker of disconsolance, no tremor of fear, no regret, and no irresolution. Powers beyond my control had brought me to room 5 at the clinic in Casablanca, and I could not have run away then even if I had wished to.

Late at night two nurses arrived, one French, one Arab. I was to be operated on later, they said. They had come to give me a preliminary injection, and in the meantime I must shave my private parts. "You have a razor? Undress, please, and shave yourself. We will wait." They sat on the table, swinging their legs, the one holding the hypodermic syringe, the other a sterilizing bowl. I undressed and took my razor, and miserably in that bare light, with the cold water from the tap and a cake of Moroccan soap, I shaved the hair from my pubic region, while the girls watched sardonically, sporadically chatting with each other. I can see them now, swinging their legs there, while I struggled uncomfortably on, a lonely naked figure in the middle of the room, where the light was brightest.

At last it was done, and they injected me upon the bed. "Go to sleep now," they said, "the operation will be later." But when they had gone I got out of bed rather shakily, for the drug was beginning to work, and went to say good-bye to myself in the mirror. We would never meet again, and I wanted to give that other self a long last look in the eye, and a wink for luck. As I did so a street vendor outside played a delicate arpeggio upon his flute, a very gentle merry sound which he repeated, over and over again, in sweet diminuendo down the street. Flights of angels, I said to myself, and so staggered back to my bed, and oblivion.

When I awoke it was pitch-dark, and there was no sound, inside or out. I was instantly alert, but when gingerly I tried to explore the condition of my body, I found I could not move a muscle. I was pinioned in some way to the bed. My arms, stretched away from my body, seemed to be strapped to the bed itself, and I no longer appeared to have any legs. I could lift my head a little, but it did no good, for the blackness was impenetrable. I might just as well be in the grave. There was absolutely no sign of life in the clinic. If I had screamed my head off nobody would have heard. I wondered mildly if something had gone terribly wrong, and I was in fact dead; but no, I was breathing all right, my mind worked, and sure enough a cautious clenching of the abdominal muscles seemed to tell me that I was heavily bandaged, perhaps tubed, down below. It seemed to me that on the whole I was alive, well, and sex-changed in Casablanca.

This stunning thought more than compensated for the nightmare sensation of my awakening, and I found that being totally unable to move was curiously relaxing. I found myself, in fact, astonishingly happy. Very soon I was wide awake, but it still appeared to be the middle of the night, so to pass the long hours till dawn I sang to myself in the darkness. Presently the sunshine came seeping through the shuttered windows, I heard the comforting sounds of the city awakening, the Moroccan warmth began to fill the little room, and at eight in the morning a nurse arrived to release me from the bed. My wrists were bruised and red, where the thongs had cut into them; but I did not care, and polished off the crossword puzzle—well, *almost* polished it off—in no time at all.

I spent two weeks in the clinic, and gradually became accustomed, as the bandages and tubes were progressively removed, to the fact that I had a new body. Now when I looked down at myself I no longer seemed a hybrid or chimera: I was all of a piece, as proportioned once again, though in a different kind, as I had been so exuberantly on Everest long before. Then I had felt lean and muscular; now I felt above all deliciously *clean*. The protuberances I had grown increasingly to detest had been scoured from me. I was made, by my own lights, normal.

I remember my days there with an affectionate lack of clarity. They seemed to loiter by, orientally. Sometimes Fatima the head nurse came to change a dressing or inject an antibiotic: a true figure of the seraglio, I thought, a big capable woman, like a Mistress of the Knives, who did her jobs methodically and dispassionately, as though she would be reporting direct to the Sultan. Once, during a particularly painful piece of postoperative manipulation, I heard her breathe the single word *"Courage!"* under her breath, but normally her face betrayed no hint of compassion or even concern. Sometimes the room maid came in, ineffectually to dust the floor and change the bed-sheets, singing a quavering Arab melody as she went about her tasks, sometimes pausing for a long moment to look vacantly out of the balcony, and sometimes confiding in me the hardships of her domestic life. The little Arabic I remembered gave me a touch of mystery, and when an enormous bunch of roses arrived for me the other maids came in to admire them, and it was rumored that I had a rich protector in Rabat—no such luck, I told them, but ah, they said knowingly, *you speak Arabic.*

Outside, above the traffic roar, I could often hear the graceful cries of the street hawkers, trailing up and down their quarter tones, and every evening the man with the flute came by, to leave his melody hanging on the air behind him like a lullaby. And once a day Dr. B—— breezed in, smoking a Gauloise, dressed for the corniche, and looking in general pretty devastating. He would sit at the end of my bed and chat desultorily of this and that—type a few slow words on my typewriter—read a headline from *The Times* in a delectable Chevalier accent—and eventually take an infinitely gentle look at his handiwork. "*Très, très bons,* you would nevair get surgery like that in England—you see, now you will be able to *write!*"

For the first few days I felt altogether alone there. Contact with the world outside was not encouraged—"We will get anything for you, you have only to ask." The bell beside my bed never did work, and when for the first time I struggled in cruel pain across the room to the door, in the corridor outside everything seemed to be dead and empty, and I could hear no movement at all. It was an eerie feeling. Later, though, when I became precariously perambulatory, and took to exploring further, or sitting in the sunshine on my balcony, I realized that I was not after all alone. There were other pilgrims at that shrine. Sometimes I heard buzzers ringing prolonged, frenzied but evidently unanswered in the night, and from the floor below, if I leant far enough over the balcony, I could occasionally hear voices.

And later still, when I was sufficiently recovered to go downstairs to have my dressings changed, I set eyes for the first time on others like me. We met each other wandering in the corridors. How many there were of us, I do not know, but we were of several varieties. We were Greek, French, American, British. We were brunette, jet black, or violent blonde. We were butch and we were beefy, and we were provocatively svelte. We ranged from the apparently scholarly to the obviously animal. Whether we were all going from male to female, or whether some of us were traveling the other way, I do not know, for we seemed to span fairly comprehensively the gamut of the genders. Some of us were clearly unsane, others were evidently rather dotty. Some spoke in unknown tongues, some said "Hi," some grinned, some merely stared, astonished perhaps to encounter at last a fellow-member of this, the ultimate club. We were like prisoners, released momentarily from our cells for interrogation, meeting at last colleagues known to us only by code or legend. We looked at each other at once as strangers and as allies, in curiosity and in innocence.

And we had this in common too: that we were all gloriously happy. Just for those few days of our lives, if never before, if never again, we felt that we had achieved fulfillment, and were ourselves. Mutilated and crippled as we were, stumbling down the corridors trailing our bandages and clutching our nightclothes, we radiated happiness. Our faces might be tight with pain, or grotesque with splodged make-up, but they were shining too with hope. To you we might have seemed like freaks or mad people, and for many of us no doubt that moment of release would prove illusory, and we would find ourselves trapped in new perplexities no less baffling, and haunted by no less agonizing doubts. But for a week or two anyway we felt pure and true, and as we trailed each other down the passage for Fatima's impassive attentions, all our conundrums seemed unraveled.

Comrades, I wish you well, wherever you are, however the harsh world uses you!

I was still in pain, and moved with difficulty, when I flew back to London, but fortunately I found myself in the next seat to a businessman from Dundee, on his way home from a business conference. I know his name because he gave me his card when we parted, but he knew nothing of me; I told him only that I had been recovering from an illness in Morocco, and he responded with great kindness. Except for Dr. B.—— he was the very first man I had met since I had been released from my own last remnants of maleness, and I thought him a most happy omen. He made me feel more fun than I was, which was all I could ask of him, and if he chances to read these words, as he takes the night train to King's Cross, or relaxes for a moment with his Scotch on the Hamburg flight, I hope he will accept my gratitude. It was a fine thing, I thought, to be returning to my own country for a fresh start, gay with champagne and good company: like a princess emancipated from her degrading disguise, or something new out of Africa.

SEVENTEEN

ALL FOR FUN? · A MANNER SUITED VIEWS OF LIFE · FEMALE SENSATIONS FORGETTING

Elizabeth welcomed me home as though nothing in particular had happened, but I was not quite out of the woods yet. Dr. B——'s craftsmanship, though aesthetically brilliant, was functionally incomplete, and I underwent two further sessions of surgery in an English nursing-home—where, complacently encouched in my spotless room like Lili Elbe before me, I thought the military-looking man who wandered around the garden in his dressing gown singing old Anglican hymns a perfect equivalent to the knife-grinder with his music in Casablanca. I did not mind these further ordeals in the least. I would have gone through the whole cycle ten times over, if the alternative had been a return to ambiguity or disguise.

Somebody asked me, when I first came home, if I had done it all for fun. "You've always looked so cheerful," he said, "and now you look like a cat that's stolen the cream." It was true that a grand sense of euphoria now overcame me, in the fulfillment of my life's desire, so that I almost began to forget the old miseries and conflicts. I knew for certain that I had done the right thing. It was inevitable and it was deeply satisfying—like a sentence which, defying its own subordinate clauses, reaches a classical conclusion in the end. It gave me a marvelous sense of calm, as though some enormous but ill-defined physical burden had been lifted from my shoulders, and when I woke each morning I felt resplendent in my liberation. I shone! I was Ariel!

I have had time now to get used to myself, but the happiness has not worn off, the sense of daily wonder has not deserted me, and it seems to me that what has happened to me, and what I have tried to describe in this book, is one of the most fascinating experiences that ever befell a human being. In some ways it was a tragedy, of course. Of course it was. All that energy gone to waste! All those years of uncertainty! A life distorted, friends bewildered, loved ones put at risk, a fine body deformed with chemicals and slashed by the knife in a distant city! Of course one would not do it for fun, and of course if I had been given the choice of a life without such complications, I would have taken it, and joined the people down the hill.

Or would I? Had it perhaps all been worth while, now to be entering, forty-five years old, a new and springlike adventure such as few people have ever known? Thirty-five years as a male, I thought, ten in between, and the rest of my life as me. I liked the shape of it.

"Every month, nay every week, witnesses further progress in Mademoiselle d'Éon. This is not surprising, since her transmutation, taking place as it does under the eyes of the court, is working miracles in her heart and mind. Being unable to show herself anywhere except in the attire of her sex, she is compelled to comport herself in a manner suited to her dress and to maintain the attitude which nature and the

King's commands have ordained for her. . . . As she feels that she is destined always to wear female dress, she brings reason to reinforce necessity in her determination to accustom herself to her situation."

So wrote Madame Genet, into whose care was placed the Chevalier d'Éon, aged forty-nine, when at the State's command he assumed the female role for the rest of his life. He was four years older than I was when I entered the same experience, and a good deal worldlier, but what happened to him, happened to me. I could only live as a woman now, and I resigned from the Travellers' Club, and gave away my dinner jacket, and wrote to *Who's Who*, and abandoned the last of my male prerogatives. Being unable to show myself anywhere, as the lady said, except in the female role, I too found changes involuntarily occurring, so that not only reason and necessity, but circumstance too combined to close the book upon my past.

Fortunately for me, the first society into which I ventured frankly and publicly sex-changed was the profoundly civilized society of Caernarvonshire. The Welsh are kind to most people, and especially kind to their own. My neighbors and friends at Trefan, the villagers of Llanystumdwy, the farmers all around, the shopkeepers of Cricieth down the road, the community of artists, writers, and philosophers who lived along the coast—all greeted my moment of metamorphosis with an urbane insouciance. It is a perturbing experience, to walk for the first time in skirts into a shop, say, whose people have known you for a male for many years, and it was instructive to see how the Welsh coped with it. Some could not restrain a kind of gasp, instantly stifled. Some tactfully said how well I looked that morning. But most, with that accomplishment of performance which is the national birthright, simply pretended not to notice, spoke to me as they always did, asked after the children, and by the skill of their pose put me at my ease, and in their debt.

On Boxing Day each year we threw the big house open to our neighbors, littering it with bottles of wine and bowls of punch, and inviting our guests to help themselves. That year, my first as a woman, my last in the house, more people came than ever, and in all our rooms, except those on whose doors children had placed stern injunctions like KEAP OUT, or PRIFAT, familiar voices sounded, familiar faces smiled. Yet though it all looked the same as ever, I knew that it was not. Everyone knew me now for what I was, and there could be no pretense. I felt my personality changing almost as I walked among my guests; and I felt them too, whether they wished it or not, adjusting their attitudes to me. This was not a displeasing sensation. It was like a parting, but a gentle parting. I expect some of those people despised me really, or mocked me behind my back, but spanning as I did in my person the races, the generations, and now even the sexes themselves, I felt more strongly than ever all their kinships with me, from the fathomless understanding of Elizabeth to the complicity of the fine old dowagers sitting tipsy on the stairs.

Elsewhere in the world the impact was more abrupt. We are told that the social gap between the sexes is narrowing, but I can only report that having, in the second half of the twentieth century, experienced life in both roles, there seems to me no aspect of existence, no moment of the day, no contact, no arrangement, no response, which is not different for men and for women. The very tone of voice in which I was now addressed, the very posture of the person next in the queue, the very feel in the air when I entered a room or sat at a restaurant table, constantly emphasized my change of status.

And if others' responses shifted, so did my own. The more I was treated as a woman, the more woman I became. I adapted willy-nilly. If I was assumed to be incompetent at reversing cars, or opening bottles, oddly incompetent I found myself becoming. If a case was thought too heavy for me, inexplicably I found it so myself. Thrust as I now found myself far more into the company of women than of men, I began to find women's conversation in general more congenial. Women treated me with a frankness which, while it was one of the happiest discoveries of my metamorphosis, did imply membership of a camp, a faction, or at least a school of thought; and so I found myself gravitating always towards the female, whether in sharing a railway compartment or supporting a political cause. Men treated me more and more as a junior, as the Chevalier d'Éon had been obliged to accept a guardian in his womanhood—my lawyer, in an unguarded moment one morning, even called me "my child"; and so, addressed every day of my life as an inferior, involuntarily, month by month I accepted the condition. I discovered that even now men prefer women to be less informed, less able, less talkative, and certainly less self-centered than they are themselves; so I generally obliged them.

It is hard for me now to remember what everyday life was like as a man—unequivocally as a man, I mean, before my change began at all. Sometimes, though, by a conscious effort I try to recapture the sensation, and realize the contrast in my condition now. It amuses me to consider, for instance when I am taken out to lunch by one of my more urbane men friends, that not so many years ago that fulsome waiter would have treated *me* as he is now treating *him*. Then he would have greeted me with respectful seriousness. Now he unfolds my napkin with a playful flourish, as if to humor me. Then he would have taken my order with grave concern, now he expects me to say something frivolous (and I do). Then he would have pretended, at least, to respect my knowledge of wines, now I am not even consulted. Then he would have addressed me as a superior, now he seems to think of me (for he is a cheerful man) as an accomplice. I am treated of course with the conventional deference that a woman expects, the moving of tables, the wrapping of coats, the opening of doors; but I know that it is really deference of a lesser kind, and that the man behind me is the guest that counts.

But it soon all came to feel only natural, so powerful are the effects of custom and environment. Late as I came in life to womanhood—"a late developer," as somebody said of me—the subtle subjection of women was catching up on me, and I was adjusting to it in just the way women have adjusted down the generations. It was, of course, by no means all unpleasant. If the condescension of men could be infuriating, the courtesies were very welcome. If it was annoying to be thought incapable of buying a second-class return to Liverpool, it was quite nice to have it done for one anyway. I did not particularly want to be good at reversing cars, and did not in the least mind being patronized by illiterate garage-men, if it meant they were going to give me some extra trading stamps.

People are usually far kinder to women, and society is more indulgent too. The parking problem is a case in point. It daunts men much more easily than it daunts women, and with reason: the man must fight for his place at the curb, the woman can be fairly sure that at a pinch somebody will let her in, or off, and that a smile and a jollity will see her through. In most of life's everyday episodes the woman enjoys similar advantages. She can speak more trenchantly, for she is less likely to be answered back, and she can take more chances, for the stupid will take her for a fool and the intelligent will respect her daring. Her frailty is her strength, her inferiority is her privilege, unless of course she is confronted by one of the more terrible London meter maidens, those walking texts of frustration, in which case Heaven alone can help her.

The more preposterous handicaps of the female state, embodied in common law as in business prejudice, are clearly doomed: nobody of sense can support them, and they are mere impertinences left over from the past. The lesser social bigotries and condescensions, and the female responses they evoke, will doubtless survive us all. They have certainly had their effect on me, an effect which Madame Genet described as "a becoming harmony between her behavior and her dress," but which in myself I see to be a kind of opportunist submission. The first man who ever kissed me, in a carnal way, after my return from Casablanca, was a London taxi-driver who drove me one morning to the recently opened Army museum in Chelsea. We chatted all the way across London, and when we reached the museum he got out of his cab to look at the new building with me. Quite suddenly, slipping his arm around my waist boldly on the pavement, he kissed me roughly and not at all disagreeably on the lips. "There's a good girl," he said, patting my bottom and returning to his cab; and all I did was blush.

These were essentially changes in attitude and response; but there were inner changes in me, too, more subtle, more important. Some were simply the psychological effects of fulfillment, but some sprang from the end of my maleness, and were more truly the symptoms of womanhood.

Physically I was no longer ambiguous of appearance. My body was no longer producing its male androgens, and the leanness left my face, indefinably changing the character of it. I filled out rather, in the cheeks, in the hips, in the bosom, and when I thought about it I found that I now walked, sat, gesticulated altogether in a woman's way. I could no longer pass as a man, even if I had wanted to, but unlike the poor Chevalier I never pined for my boots and buckler. On the contrary, crossing this physiological line seemed to set a comforting seal upon my past, and cut me off from it emotionally too. I wish I could say I retained that second youth I had enjoyed in my epicene days, but as a woman, alas, the years pursued me again, and I looked about my chronological age. I was less striking as a female than I had been as a male, at least in the last months of my manhood; on the other hand I found that my new happiness was infectious, and I struck up friendships more easily, and plucked more instant chords of empathy. I was desperately anxious that my children should not be ashamed of me; if they were they never showed it, while Elizabeth professed it only a relief, to be in my true company at last.

Psychologically I was distinctly less forceful. A neurotic condition common among women is called penis envy, its victims supposing that there is inherent to the very fact of the male organs some potent energy of the spirit. There is something to this fancy. It is not merely the loss of androgens that has made me more retiring, more ready to be led, more passive: the removal of the organs themselves has contributed, for there was to the presence of the penis something positive, thrusting, and muscular. My body then was made to push and initiate, it is made now to yield and accept, and the outside change has had its inner consequences.

Though I found myself now far less introspective, so that writing this book was to be a difficult self-discipline for an all too facile writer, yet I became a more private person too. I cared less for the opinions of others, and I was able to subsist more easily on my own resources. Women are more self-contained than men, and at heart less gregarious. In the ladies' room they are far less likely to exchange conversation with strangers than the men are across the way: watch two women asked to share a restaurant table, and the chances are that, beyond a polite murmuring of "Would you mind?" they will not speak to each other from soup to sherry trifle. As a man I would have found such a situation absurd, being an inveterate talker in railway carriages and aircraft; as a woman I often found it rather a relief, and like the Arab lady retreating into the black anonymity of the veil, often cosseted myself in privacy.

My view of life shifted too. I was even more emotional now. I cried very easily, and was ludicrously susceptible to sadness or flattery. Finding myself rather less interested in great affairs (which are placed in a new perspective, I do assure you, by a change of sex), I acquired a new concern for small ones. My scale of vision seemed to contract, and I looked less for the grand sweep than for the telling detail. The emphasis changed in my writing, from places to people. The specious topographical essay which had been my *forte*, and my income, became less easy for me to write, and I found myself concentrating more on individuals or situations. Throughout the years of my change I was deeply engaged, though you might not guess it from this highly selective memoir, upon my most ambitious work, a trilogy about the Victorian Empire. The first volume I wrote while I was still a man, and it was above all an evocation of an era, and a world; the second I wrote during the last years of my metamorphosis, and it is far richer in personalities and episodes; the third I have not started yet, and I await its character with interest. Just as I feel emancipated as a person, so I do as a writer; perhaps I shall be a novelist yet.

For while the androgynous condition was a positive asset in reportage, it disqualified me for fiction. From the beginning of my life I had felt that my state of detachment gave me a privileged view of things—a seat in the Royal Enclosure, or a two-way mirror. It was hardly an objective view, for I saw everything through the lens of my introspections, but it was always uninvolved. I shared, or allowed myself to share, so few of the emotions I described; I felt myself outside mankind's preoccupations; I was a good reporter, because I was tightly circumscribed, like a race horse blinkered against distractions, with its fierce eyes always on the winning-post. But when it came to literature more creative, I felt myself ham-strung. The book I am writing now is my very first attempt at a more liberated self-expression. Of course it is all about myself, and does not reach the ultimate freedom of fiction, but at least it is more than mere observation. For I no longer feel myself isolated and unreal. Not only can I imagine more vividly now how other people feel: released at last from those old bridles and blinkers, I am beginning to know how I feel myself.

It is, I think, a simpler vision that I now possess. Perhaps it is nearer a child's. I can more easily see things for the first time, as it were, stripping them of cross-reference—and this is a startling sensation, for twenty years of the writer's trade clutters one's view with comparisons. Colors seem brighter than they did, and if I take more interest in clothes, mine and other people's, it is partly because I have much more fun in wearing them, and live perpetually on the brink of appalling extravagances, but partly because I now value first impressions more, and am not so anxious to move on to allusion and interpretation. All my life I had never been able to understand that particular visual fancy which, looking down at the passing cars from an airplane or a church tower, sees them as toys. They never looked like toys to me, only like real cars seen from a great distance, so that they seemed small. No longer. On a flight to Dublin a few months ago suddenly the scales dropped from my eyes, and looking through the aircraft window upon the English scene beneath, lo! I had acquired the sight of children, and saw it all as dolls' houses and Dinky toys.

You are wondering how I now saw men and women. Clearly, I would say, for the first time. I had no inhibitions, no half-conscious restraints. Nor was I atrophied now, for I felt the sexual urges cheerfully revived. Looking back at my old persona, I sadly recognized my own frustrated desires, plain at last, but irretrievably wasted. I saw how deeply I had pined for the arms and the love of a man. I saw how proud and brave a wife I would like to have been, how passionate a mother, how forlornly my poor self had yearned to be released into its full sexuality—that flowering which, *faute de mieux*, I had so often redirected into words, or patriotism, or love of place. The shutters were removed at last, no longer clamped down, like those clanking steel blinds of the Cairo shopkeepers, to keep the unwanted at bay during the long siesta. I was walking along Jermyn Street one day when I saw, for the first time in twenty years, a member of the Everest team of 1953. My goodness, I said to myself, what an extraordinarily handsome man. I knew he had been handsome all along, but I had allowed myself to like him only for his gentle manners, and it was only now that I permitted myself the indulgence of thinking him desirable.

I had found my own level, and looking frankly around me at the human species, admitted at last without embarrassment how attractive men could be, and what a pleasure it was to be cherished by them. At last I look at them with my sexuality unbound, and my attitude unpretending. I am asked sometimes if I plan to marry one, but no, the men I have loved are married already, or dead, or far away, or indifferent. Too late! Besides, though Elizabeth and I are divorced, we are locked in our friendship more absolutely than ever, and unless some blinding passion intervenes with one or the other of us, propose to share our lives happily ever after. She has a farmhouse in the Black Mountains of South Wales; I have a flat in Bath; we share the old buildings at Trefan; and linking us always wherever we are, and connecting us too with our children near and far, is a dear bond we cannot break.

"What does it feel like to be a woman, after so many years as a man?" I cannot honestly answer this familiar question. For one thing I never thought myself to be truly a man, and do not know how a man feels. For another, there are aspects of being a woman that I shall never experience—girlhood, menstruation, childbirth, an unequivocal female sexualness. And for a third, nobody really knows how anybody else feels—you may think you are feeling as a woman, or as a man, but you may simply be feeling as yourself.

But let me analyze myself, on an ordinary morning in

Bath, where I go to write my books. Let me see what everyday, inessential sensations I conceive as specifically female. First, I feel small, and neat. I am not small in fact, at 5′ 9″ and 133 lbs., and not terribly neat either, but femininity conspires to make me feel so. My blouse and skirt are light, bright, crisp. My shoes make my feet look more delicate than they are, besides giving me, perhaps more than any other piece of clothing, a suggestion of vulnerability that I rather like. My red and white bangles give me a racy feel, my bag matches my shoes and makes me feel well organized. I do not use make-up much, but what there is on my face is enlivening, fun, like a fresh lick of paint on a front door. When I walk out into the street I feel consciously ready for the world's appraisal, in a way that I never felt as a man.

And when the news agent seems to look at me with approval, or the man in the milk-cart smiles, I feel absurdly elated, as though I have been given a good review in the *Sunday Times*. I know it is nonsense, but I cannot help it. My moods and conditions are more variable now, and an early touch of flattery, I have discovered, starts a chain reaction, and lasts the whole day through. I am well aware that these fluctuations really come from within, not from the reactions of milkman and news vendor, but in a curious way my inner sensations show on the outside, and set the postman smiling too. I don't believe men feel this instant contact with the world around them; for me it is one of the constant fascinations and stimulants of my new condition.

What do I notice, on my way down the hill to the shops? Perhaps not quite so dreamily as I once did the perspectives of square and crescent; instead, the interiors of houses, glimpsed through the curtains, the polished knockers, the detail of architrave or nameplate. I look at the place more intimately, perhaps because I feel myself integral to the city's life at last. I am no longer the utterly detached, the almost alienated observer of the scene; I am one with it, linked by an eager empathy with the homelier things about it, the life of kitchen and garden, the children and the pets, shopping and unimportant talk. This is good for my morale, but may in time alter the nature, I think, of what in pretentious moments I call my art.

I stop for a gossip. Not at all a feline gossip, as I might have shared in the 9th Lancers, at Printing House Square, or even at a shamefaced pinch with colleagues of the *Guardian*, but a gentle, harmless, fairly meaningless, meandering gossip. I am conscious that this conversation lacks form or substance, but I enjoy it anyway. It is a tranquilizing ritual, rather like knitting, sustained by stylized conventional phrases of pleasure or complaint, as in a Kabuki drama, but in its transient way sincere. "Surely you must get sick to death," a male acquaintance wrote to me the other day, "of the conversation of your new peers"; but in fact the longer I spend in my new state of life, the more I enjoy meeting Mrs. Weatherby on the way to the shops.

She really is concerned, though my acquaintance would probably disbelieve it, about my migraine yesterday; and when I examine myself I find that I am no less genuinely distressed to hear that Amanda missed the school outing because of her ankle. I am no better a person than I used to be, but in little matters I am nicer. I care rather more, perhaps because I am less obsessed with myself. I can place myself more easily in Mrs. Weatherby's situation. I am more truly interested. Would I feel the same if I were gossiping with a man? Probably not. I would take his sincerity with a pinch of salt, and I would be slightly on guard myself.

I cultivate no instincts of economy, and have little interest in food, so I spend my time at the food store perfunctorily, a couple of chops to shove beneath the grill, the first lettuce I see, loads of the best Cox's, spring onions, radishes, Camembert, and a bagful of shelled Brazils. A lady I know observes pointedly that apples are cheaper in George Street, but life seems to me too short for a penny in the pound, and to make my point I eat one on the spot. I spend much longer window-shopping. None of life's changes or catastrophes, of course, will ever keep me out of the bookshops, an addiction that ignores sex or gender, but in a totally new way now I like browsing through other things. I love looking at clothes, trying them on too, even if I have no real intention of buying anything. I like looking at carpets, and wallpapers, not to speak of antiques, furniture, pictures, or houses—no longer, as I used to, only when I have a purpose in mind, but simply for the pleasure of doing it. I buy a construction kit for Tom at the toyshop, fondly fancying his eyes when he opens it; and then, imagining Susan's crestfallen little face behind him, I buy her something too.

It is distinctly a woman's world that I inhabit in Bath. I never lived there as a man myself, and my everyday contact with men is brief and essentially artificial, both sides playing a part. My contact with women, on the other hand, is easy and confiding. I am asked often if this has made me a militant feminist, and in some ways it has. I have seen life from both sides, and I know what prejudice survives. I know that by the very fact of my womanhood, even in so urbane a city as Bath, I am treated in many petty situations as a second-class citizen—not because I lack brains, or experience, or character, but purely because I wear the body of a woman. Nothing infuriates me more than to see a woman brushed aside or scorned by some dullard man (intelligent men, of course, never do it); for I know for absolute certain how nonsensical this bigotry is, and I boil to think of it applied to greater affairs of life.

So I well understand what Kipling had in mind, about sisters under the skin. Over coffee a lady from Montreal effuses about Bath—"I don't know if you've done any traveling yourself" (not *too* much, I demurely lie) "but I do feel it's important, don't you, to see how other people *really* live." I bump into Jane W—— in the street, and she tells me about Archie's latest excess—"Honestly, Jan, you don't know how lucky you are." I buy some typing-paper—"How lovely to be able to write, you make me feel a proper *dunce*"—and walking home again to start work on a new chapter, find that workmen are in the flat, taking down a picture-rail. One of them has knocked my little red horse off the mantelpiece, chipping its enameled rump. I restrain my annoyance, summon a fairly frosty smile, and make them all cups of tea, but I am thinking to myself, as they sheepishly help themselves to sugar, a harsh feminist thought. It would be a man, I think.

Well it would, wouldn't it?

Such are the superficials of my new consciousness—and despite the little red horse I must add to them a frank enjoyment, which I think most honest women will admit to, of the small courtesies men now pay me, the standing up or the opening of doors, which really do give one a cherished or protected feeling, undeserved perhaps but very welcome. Deeper new emotions I find it much harder to isolate, and this is not merely because they are more elusive, but because I am fast forgetting what I felt before the change. The past is receding more than usually quickly, and I am losing the last comparisons: the male stride, the male assurance, the problems and perquisites of malehood, the constancy and the strength, the independence, the supremacy. I cannot really remember how I would have talked to Mrs. Weatherby then. I cannot imagine what Jane would have said about Archie. I am forgetting it all fast: partly because each month I become more accustomed to my womanhood, and partly because I do not want to remember.

EIGHTEEN

PROBLEMS STILL · ASK A SILLY QUESTION · "ONE IS BAFFLED" REGRETS?

"If a man can so inoculate himself with the idea that he is not a man, but a woman, as to be to all intents and purposes a woman, that idea may in turn be made to give way to a higher ideal—that there is neither man nor woman."

This quotation was sent to me by Henry from India, and it greatly comforted me, for of the problems that remained to me after Casablanca, much the most serious concerned my children. I would not know how these unusual events would affect them—nor shall I know, I suppose, for years to come. But at least I had not antagonized them. All four had been my staunchest allies throughout the change, screening me, supporting me, reassuring me, and nobody could be more punctiliously reproving than Susan, when some old acquaintance used the wrong personal pronoun of me. They knew how infinitely I cherished them in return, and the older two at least, now men themselves, were strong and wise enough, I knew, to look beyond sex for truth—"Ponder deeply," as another of Henry's quotations said, "and thou shalt know that there is no such thing as I." It was not such a terrible thing, after all. They had not witnessed the collapse of love, the betrayal of parentage, desertion or dislike. What they had watched was a troubled soul achieving serenity, and I hoped that in time they would come to see in my strange life, as I have seen it, some unexpected flicker of *baraka*.

Mark, the eldest, has read every word of this book in its successive drafts, and besides powerfully influencing its shape and character, has illuminated my task with cheerful perspectives of his own. It so happened that in the course of the work King Gustav of Sweden died. It was he, you may remember, who was reported to me in Chapter Twelve as plotting my sex-change by secret rays, and in the margin of my typescript Mark added his own comment on the news: *"Clearly the success of Gustav's machinations was too much for the old boy."*

As for myself, my difficulties now seemed petty. I had reached Identity. To my family and closest friends, I knew, the physical change would make no difference, imperceptibly gradual as it had been, and most other people too seemed predisposed to accept me for myself. Even the Press was indulgent. When news agencies or American magazines rang up, I told them what I reasonably could and asked them, since the time to reveal everything was inopportune, and since after all I did have the happiest memories of that lunch we shared while covering Churchill's illness in the south of France, if they would mind spiking the story. Most of them obligingly did, perhaps on the principle that sensible dogs don't bite dogs, and being fairly jaded with sex-change stories anyway. From time to time wan local journalists, having heard the bizarre tale through the grapevine of country gossip, nervously drove up to Trefan to ask for interviews; but I persuaded them always that it was dead news, and not very sensational either, and they generally drove away with a perceptible sigh of relief, as though they had stood on the brink of the unknown, but had been snatched back just in time. The only interviewer who did throw me off my balance was an exceedingly clever and delightful girl from London, who besides being a detective's daughter, and thus adept at the unnerving silence, knew far more about transsexualism than I did myself, and capped my every speculation with a proven statistic, or still worse a fact.

So I was able to change my public identity in my own time. Presently I took to signing articles and reviews as Jan; also letters to *The Times*, whose letters editor imperturbably printed them, through the sequence of male to female, without comment. By the end of 1973, I discovered, most people who would have heard of me anyway knew of my change of sex, both in England and in America, and those who were not sure whether to address me as Mrs., Miss, or just Jan were fortunately able to fall back upon a prefix recently and usefully devised, Ms.—just the thing, so everybody thought, for the likes of me.

The response to this cautious self-revelation was encouraging. People I had not seen for years wrote to wish me well. Editors politely asked me in which persona I now wished to be published, and a courteous functionary from the Ministry, coming to Trefan to give me my new insurance card, apologetically explained that the question of my retirement pension would have to be settled nearer the time (women get theirs earlier than men, and I suppose he thought I might change back again). As my confidence grew, I devised new techniques for dealing with the complex social demands now made upon me—when to reveal all, when to let things go, how to discover what people already knew, when best to tackle an old acquaintance who, glimpsed through a sea of heads at a literary reception, was evidently unsure whether it was really I, or some Martini hallucination. My new name, though just right for me, I thought, was sometimes itself confusing. "I thought Jan Morris was a man," said a jolly Australian at a *Spectator* lunch one day. "What happened, d'you change your sex or something?" Just that, I replied. Ask a silly question and you get a footling answer.

Gradually, on these terms, the range of my ease widened. Among all the hundreds of our acquaintances, only one true-blue Yorkshireman made me feel that my presence in his house would be an embarrassment, or vice versa. I was received with curiosity by most people, with amusement by some, with nonchalance by dons and aristocrats, with kindly incomprehension by soldiers and old ladies, with earnestness by those who wanted to demonstrate their enlightenment, with a flourish by those who relished a nine-day wonder at their dinner tables, with bold kisses by extroverts, with shy circumspection by people who wanted to confide in me, over the coffee, their own little problems of personality. Finally, to cap this social reincarnation, I was taken to dinner at the ladies' end of the Travellers' Club dining room, one of my favorite rooms in London, which lies chandeliered and portraited paralled with Pall Mall, illuminated on days of State ceremonial by the six gas flambeaux which blaze and flurry outside. This was a curious occasion by any standards, and unique I would dare to claim in the long history of London clubs.

It was a happy evening for me. My host was an old friend, the wine was better than I ever ordered for myself, and the staff of the club, who had known me for so long in one guise, welcomed me without a flicker in the other—only the wine waiter betraying, in a faint gleam of his hooded eye as he poured me another glass, a hint of amused collusion. I had always admired the London clubman who boasted of himself that he had experienced all the pleasures mankind was heir to, except only the joys of childbirth; but I could not help feeling, as we moved on to the green figs with cream, my favorite in that room during so many years of manhood, that I had beaten him at his own game.

Few people understood it. I did not expect them to understand the cause, since it was a mystery even to me, but I had supposed more people might understand the compulsion. I had once surmised that it might be an impulse common to all male persons, and though friends of both sexes vehemently deny it, it still seems to me only common sense to wish to be a woman rather than a man—or if not common sense, at least good taste.

Those who easily accepted the proposition were mostly women themselves. Sometimes, perhaps, this was paradoxically because they had once themselves wished to be men—in a dilettante sort of way, a common enough inclination. More often it was because, being happy themselves, well balanced in their gender, unconfused, they well appreciated why I would wish to be the same. It would seem odious to them to be condemned to manhood, and they saw that it was odious for me. Among such people, whose company I have come to enjoy more than any other, I have found myself not merely understood, but positively welcomed to womankind.

Many men, on the other hand, and less well-integrated women professed themselves stupefied. "This is very strange," was a typical observation on the first draft of this manuscript—"one is baffled"—"how *could* it be?" It was generally because they read my tale always as a parable of sex, looking in it for reflections or explanations of their own sexual preferences, and finding, when they hoped for sperm, orgasms, or erections, only frogs in an Oxford meadow, or Egyptian jasmine. They looked for lust; but though my life has been a life of lust, lust of the loins has been a lesser part of it, and has not been the thread of this story.

Occasionally, especially among the cruder kind of men, I have sensed an element of resentment in this blockage. It is almost as though I have let them down. More often, though, among women as well as men, I have detected envy. They wrongly suppose that I have chosen my own path. They think I have been doubly free. They quote to me W. E. Henley:

I am the master of my fate:
I am the captain of my soul.

when they should be quoting Cecil Day Lewis:

Tell them in England, if they ask
What brought us to these wars,
To this plateau beneath the night's
Grave manifold of stars—

It was not fraud or foolishness,
Glory, revenge, or pay:
We came because our open eyes
Could see no other way.

I am often asked if I have any regrets, and I answer frivolously no, except that I seem to have lost some of the pleasures of wine drinking, and wish I could still consult the railway timetables at the Travellers. But of course I have regrets. I regret the shock I have given to others. I regret lost time. Occasionally I regret my manhood, when it comes to getting a job done properly, or having my opinion listened to. I regret the necessity of it all, just as I regret the stolen years of completeness, as man or as woman, that might have been mine.

But I do not for a moment regret the act of change. I could see no other way, and it has made me happy. In this I am one of the lucky few. There are people of many kinds who have set out on the same path, and by and large they are among the unhappiest people on the face of the earth. Since I went to Casablanca I have met some, and corresponded with many more. Some have achieved surgery, some merely pine for it, and every complication of the sexual urge, every tangle of social neurosis, is to be found somewhere in their anxieties. I know a university lecturer, born male, who underwent surgery without any hormonal preliminaries because he wished to live as a lesbian. I know a distinguished and exquisitely cultured civil servant, now in his late fifties, whose life has been wrecked by his bitter jealousy of womanhood—his confidence shattered by terrible aversion treatment, his powerful physique transformed by hormones, his marriage broken, his career abandoned. I know of an educated woman, converted to malehood, so terrified of her new role that she has forsaken home, family, and all, and shut herself up in loneliness in a distant country town. And these are clever, articulate people; I do not speak of all the poor castaways of intersex, the misguided homosexuals, the transvestites, the psychotic exhibitionists, who tumble through this half-world like painted clowns, pitiful to others and often horrible to themselves.

Sex has its reasons too, but I suspect the only transsexuals who can really achieve happiness are those of the classic kind, the lifelong puzzlers, to whom it is not primarily a sexual dilemma at all—who offer no rational purpose to their compulsions, even to themselves, but are simply driven blindly and helplessly towards the operating table. Of all our fellows, we are the most resolute. Nothing will stop us, no fear of ridicule or poverty, no threat of isolation, not even the prospect of death itself. During my years of torment I generally found it safer (for I did not wish to risk my sanity more than I could help) to approach my problem existentially, and to assume that it was altogether of itself, *sans* cause, *sans* meaning. It is only in writing this book that I have delved so deeply into my own emotions. Yet nothing I have discovered there has shaken my conviction, and if I were trapped in that cage again nothing would keep me from my goal, however fearful its prospect, however hopeless the odds. I would search the earth for surgeons, I would bribe barbers or abortionists, I would take a knife and do it myself, without fear, without qualms, without a second thought.

NINETEEN

THE HUMAN CONDITION SPECULATIONS · UNDER THE PIANO STILL

Images of magic have abounded in this book, wizards and wise women, miracles and virgin birth. I interpreted my journey from the start as a quest, sacramental or visionary, and in retrospect it has assumed for me a quality of epic, its purpose unyielding, its conclusion inevitable.

I am well aware, though, that to others the story will seem very different, less heroic than peculiar, with its central figure not so much inspired as half daft. For me an enigma lies at the root of my dilemma, and I am content to leave it so; others may hope for a more exact diagnosis, and would prefer me to worry the problem further still, pursuing its echo down the paneled corridors of psychiatry, or looking for its shade in halls of social science. Acquaintances often treat me as a sounding board for their own neuroses, just as many readers will doubtless have read this book hoping for sidelights on their own confusions.

I made a first attempt at writing it years ago during a visit to Russia, and when I left the country for Finland the customs official at Leningrad, searching my possessions, came across the manuscript. He looked at it with suspicion, but after reading a few sentences nodded his head sagely. "Ah," he said, "a psychological novel, I see"—and returning it to my case he gestured me through the barrier with respect. Many people believe that what has happened to me reflects more than a rare predicament, but in some way illustrates *la condition humaine*, like a Dostoevsky story; and perhaps it does.

Certainly some of my conflicts have been conflicts of the general. There is, for example, the conflict of self-determination—the degree to which a human being is entitled to choose his own identity. I felt a slight chill when the man from the Ministry, delivering my new social security card, showed me my own dossier, taped and sealed with wax, ready to be delivered to the national register at Newcastle. "Nobody," he said, "will be allowed to look inside that file without special permission"—but I noticed that he did not invite me to see inside it, either. I sometimes feel that I have struck a small blow for liberty, changing my persona in a Moroccan boulevard; but at other times it occurs to me that one day the man from the Ministry, drawing upon such precedents, may feel entitled to choose our persona for us, to seal in that dossier not just a discarded pension card, but ourselves.

Then again I wonder if, by denying physical sex a supreme importance in my life (for such of course must be one moral of my epic) I am ahead of my time. I notice that a change of sex surprises and excites the middle-aged far more than the young, and I wonder if this means that sex is past its heyday. It has long lost the sanctity it commanded in our grandmothers' day. Degraded by publicity, made casual by tolerance, defused by post-Freudian psychiatry, made unnecessary by artificial insemination, it is already becoming a matter not of the spirit but of the mechanism. Hymen has lost its mystery. Babies may be prevented or aborted, as you will. Boys and girls mingle promiscuously, only switching on their sexual roles, it seems, when the urge arises. Sexual intercourse will always remain a pleasure, of course, but I suspect it will become a pleasure entirely functional, like eating or drinking; and I am not the first to discover that one recipe for an idyllic marriage is a blend of affection, physical potency, and sexual incongruity.

Gender is a different matter. I foresee the day when scientists can evolve a reproductive system of choice, so that parents or more likely Governments can decree the sex of anyone, or organize the sexual balance of society. It will be harder to systematize gender. It is a more nebulous entity, however you conceive it. It lives in cavities. It cannot be computerized or tabulated. It transcends the body as it defies the test tube, yet the consciousness of it can be so powerful that it can drive someone like me relentlessly and unerringly through every stage of life.

I have collated it with the medieval idea of soul; but I am prepared to concede that one's sense of gender may be partly acquired, as the psychologists say, or at least powerfully influenced by the state of society. Would my conflict have been so bitter if I had been born now, when the gender line is so much less rigid? If society had allowed me to live in the gender I preferred, would I have bothered to change sex? Is mine only a transient phenomenon, between the dogmatism of the last century, when men were men and women were ladies, and the eclecticism of the next, when citizens will be free to live in the gender role they prefer? Will people read of our pilgrimage to Casablanca, a hundred years hence, as we might read of the search for the philosopher's stone, or Simeon Stylites on his pillar?

I hope so. For every transsexual who grasps that prize, Identity, ten, perhaps a hundred discover it to be only a mirage in the end, so that their latter quandary is hardly less terrible than their first.

But I think not, because I believe the transsexual urge, at least as I have experienced it, to be far more than a social compulsion, but biological, imaginative, and essentially spiritual, too. On a physical plane I have myself achieved, as far as is humanly possible, the identity I craved. Distilled from those sacramental fancies of my childhood has come the conviction that the nearest humanity approaches to perfection is in the persons of good women—and especially perhaps in the persons of kind, intelligent, and healthy women of a certain age, no longer shackled by the mechanisms of sex but creative still in other kinds, aware still in their love and sensuality, graceful in experience, past ambition but never beyond aspiration. In all countries, among all races, on the whole these are the people I most admire: and it is into their ranks, I flatter myself, if only in the rear file, if only on the flank, that I have now admitted myself.

But if my sense of isolation has gone, my sense of difference remains, and this is inevitable. However skillful Dr. B—, however solicitous the Department of Health and Social Security, I can never be as other people. My past is with me, and there is more to come. For to my journey there was always that trace of mysticism, madness if you will, and the unity I sought, I know now, was more than a unity of sex and gender, and reached towards the further vision that Henry saw for me: "a higher ideal—that there is neither man nor woman."

So I do not mind my continuing ambiguity. I have lived the life of man, I live now the life of woman, and one day perhaps I shall transcend both—if not in person, then perhaps in art, if not here, then somewhere else. There is no norm, no criterion, and perhaps no explanation. What if I remain an equivocal figure? I think of the man who touched doors in Kampur, armored in his strangeness; I think of the herons I used to catch poaching on the river at Trefan, so solitary, so angular, so self-sufficient; I remember the Kenya wart-hogs, "beautiful to each other"; and looking at my continuing loves, amazed still at the universal sensuality of life, I reach the conclusion that there is nobody in the world I would rather be than me. "Today," says a Californian slogan I admire, "is the first day of the rest of your life!"

Yet I know it to be partly illusion, and sometimes if I stand back and look at myself dispassionately, as I looked that night in the mirror at Casablanca—if I consider my story in detachment I sometimes seem, even to myself, a figure of fable or allegory. I am reminded then of the African hunter and the forbidden room, and I see myself not as man or woman, self or other, fragment or whole, but only as that wondering child with a cat beneath the Blüthner—which is mine now, by the way, but which plays not a bar of Sibelius from one year to the next, none of us being accomplished enough to tackle that master.